When Wisdom Blooms

Awaken The Sage Within

Alex P. Keats

Right Now
Publishing

Right Now Publishing
ISBN - 13: 978-0615940373
ISBN - 10: 0615940374

First Printing, 2012
Printed in the United States of America

Other Books by Alex P. Keats:

Born To Be Happy
How To Uncover Your Natural State Of Happiness

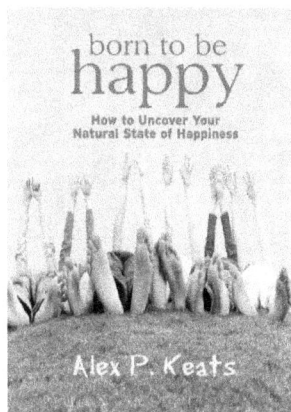

If we really are born to be happy, then why is it so elusive to so many of us? Is happiness really dependent upon the circumstances in our lives - or is there more to it than that? How do our beliefs and our past affect our ability to be truly happy? *"Born To Be Happy - How to Uncover Your Natural State of Happiness"* by Alex P. Keats, explores these questions in depth and will help you discover how to live in harmony with the happiness that's already your natural state.

Tapping into both ancient wisdom and your inner wisdom that already knows what's true, you'll understand why so many methods and strategies for happiness are short-lived and fleeting. As a result, you'll be armed with the knowledge that opens the floodgates to your natural state of happiness ... and your life will never be the same.

The Dance of Imperfection
Living in Perfect Harmony with Life

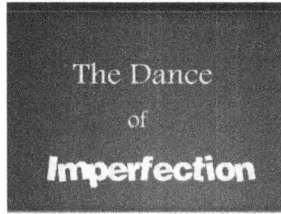

The Dance

of

Imperfection

Living in
Perfect Harmony
with Life

Alex P. Keats

Conventional wisdom would have us believe perception is reality, and that if we believe a thing about ourselves, it must be true. However, for anything to exist, for anything to be real, it must be present and observable. In other words, we must have the ability to validate its existence in our experience – and not just simply in our minds. Just because we perceive something to be real, doesn't mean it's real, does it? The fact is, we give all kinds of false concepts existence – and we suffer.

The antidote is simple and profound, and it takes literally no effort on our part. The solution is to question whether there is, or has ever been such a thing as "defects" in our character, or "flaws" in our makeup. What tells us this? Can we absolutely know this is true? Aside from in our perceptual interpretations, where is it? If we can't find it upon the closest examination, why do we insist on giving life to something that has no existence in reality, *especially* if it hurts?

Once the idea of imperfection was believed in, we've spent so much time and energy towards compensating for, and running from our self-perceptions we assume to be real. We've wasted so much energy entertaining and believing in the mind's assertions like, "I'm not good enough," "Others have it, but I don't," and "If only I could get rid of my faults, then I'd be happy and secure," instead of examining their reality in the first place.

Like a house of cards, it all collapses when the plug is pulled on the notion that there's actually a valid reason to feel insecure and unworthy! It all collapses when we root out and sever the main belief that says, "Imperfection is a fact of existence we all have to cope with!"

Only when we re-examine what we've been told, and only when we investigate and see it's not just a matter of semantics, will we allow ourselves to authentically embrace all of who we are. No longer do we engage in mind strategies that continue to reinforce the basic error. Free from the need to compensate for, or distract ourselves from our once-perceived imperfections, the desire to bolster or cultivate *anything* drops away. We simply enjoy life, living spontaneously from being – in perfect harmony with life.

Dedication

This book is dedicated to the objects of my affection: the 210 acres of The Ellis Preserve in Newtown Square, Pennsylvania. Even though you don't have to try, the perfection and majesty of your presence truly inspired this author. And to Momma groundhog and your three babies: Thank you for grazing less than ten feet from me, week in and week out, trusting I would bring you no harm. Your trust was well placed; what you are, I am. To harm you and your babies would be to harm myself. My deepest appreciation goes out to you and your kin.

"The foolish reject what they see, not what they think; the wise reject what they think, not what they see."

~ **Huang Po**

Contents

Introduction

This isn't a book about how to make you feel better, wiser or more spiritual. And it's certainly not a book meant to add to your current level of knowledge. It's a book that is intimately practical and engaging in the sense that it's more about how to live our lives more openly and directly, without relying on belief or past experience. It's about looking at the ways in which we unconsciously cover over our natural state of wisdom, and discover the ways in which wisdom naturally blooms.

Indeed, it is about awakening the sage within, while being fully human and down to earth. It's an invitation to look within, unabashedly – and see what tendencies are hurtful and divisive, and once and for all, transcend those tendencies without going to battle with them. It's an invitation to recognize the value of words and concepts as a means for going *beyond* words and concepts, entirely to the direct realization of reality or truth. Reality is so much more immense than any conceptual framework we can come up with, so it's best not to cling to the words in the traditional ways we've been taught.

Rather, look beyond the words to where the words point – for wisdom, truth and freedom are beyond the words. In speaking about wisdom, it implies that its opposite quality, ignorance, needs to be examined as well. Taking a closer look into the ways we unconsciously erect barriers that block our natural state of wisdom is one of the chief aims of this book.

As there's no up without down, there's no wisdom without ignorance. Ignorance *ignores* truth or reality. Identifying the barriers *to* wisdom gives us the ability to tear them down. In actuality, we can't decide to tear them down, like we decide to tear down a wall in our living room blocking our view of the backyard garden. When we *see* what's really true, and when we recognize what's really been running our lives, those barriers come down by themselves. Being conscious drives out the false; being un-conscious lets in the false. Make no mistake about it; once these barriers are identified and deconstructed, our natural state of wisdom reveals itself.

Like the intelligent farmer who knows the proper conditions must be met in order to realize a plentiful harvest, we need to realize the kind of soil in which wisdom blooms. How can we live our lives in harmony with life, and not from the mind's longings, aversions and biases that invariably lead to struggle and strife? How can we meet the moment as it actually unfolds, rather than how we wish or hope it unfolds? If *seeing* what's true, rather than believing what's true makes all the difference in our experience, in which direction do we look? How do we know we're even looking in the direction where wisdom resides, and where wisdom ultimately blossoms?

If wisdom really is fully present and available within each one of us, why does it seem so elusive and difficult to be in tune with? What might happen if we suspend all that we know for a time – and set aside everything we've accumulated in the past, for the very real possibility of experiencing a different reality, right now?

What might happen when we approach concepts we may have already been exposed to, in a very different manner – a manner without any conclusions, expectations or reference to the mind to tell us what's real and true? Whether it's from a direct question or by looking in a particular direction, when we simply allow the answers to arise, honestly and truthfully, a light is shined on the underlying beliefs and assumptions that maintain personal suffering.

The common thread throughout is one of *seeing* and *realizing*, not thinking, believing and evaluating. To *see* is to realize what's true. Unless we *see* (not with our physical eyes, but with our nonphysical awareness) and *realize*, we're just deluding ourselves. Wisdom is found below the neck; conceptual knowledge in the form of thinking, judging, comparing and calculating, is done above the neck. If it's wisdom we're after, by default, truth automatically stands at the front of the line. Without hydrogen, there's no water. Without truth, there's no wisdom. Sometimes we discover that posing a question, or looking in a particular direction, isn't meant to elicit a conceptual response from the mind.

Rather, questions can serve as a catalyst to experience, in our being, what it's like to rest in the question itself. The purpose is to facilitate an opening so that you can explore deeply within yourself the beliefs, concepts and opinions you have assumed to be real and true – and which until now might have gone unquestioned. Looking in the direction suggested by the question gives us the opportunity to see what arises from beyond the mind – for both wisdom and truth aren't realized *in* the mind. It is in this looking and resting (without any intent to answer the question conceptually) that allows us the opportunity to see clearly what hasn't been seen before.

Delving deeper into the book, you'll discover how to discern truth from falsehood, why your mind creates and maintains its stories – and ultimately, how to break free from the train of thought and let wisdom bloom. Living from your inner sage is your birthright, and your natural inheritance; claim what's already yours. Since the mind can't see or discover this, YOU'LL be reminded how to look in such a way that wisdom blooms – and you'll know when the mind is trying to usurp this looking. Don't be surprised if you find yourself void of any knowledge or conceptual understanding. It is in this aware empty space, devoid of any conceptual knowledge, that "your answer" may be realized. Only when we allow ourselves not to know, does Truth reveal itself as that which is eternally present.

Only when we empty our cup can it be filled. Only when we're willing to unlearn can we really begin to know. I invite you to read the words to follow unlike any other time, with an open heart and mind, allowing them to penetrate you in ways never experienced before. It is my sincere hope that you take full advantage of this opportunity and let your answers flow, unedited from your mind. You may want to put the book down at certain points throughout – and write them down. There's something powerful in putting words to paper.

When Wisdom Blooms – Awaken the Sage Within consists of seven chapters, with each chapter building on the previous, challenging and re-examining habitual patterns of thinking and unconscious ways of being. Instead of blindly following tradition, hearsay, religious text – or any other "authoritative" outside source, this is a book that encourages you to look and *see* for yourself what is true. The conditioned beliefs we unconsciously cling to, and the habitual tendency to seek outsides of ourselves for happiness are examined in depth.

The opportunity available within these pages is to examine the inherent pain and suffering in the mind's endless pursuit of pleasure and avoidance of pain. The point isn't to fix or change anything, but instead, to recognize what's really driving the bus. When we finally recognize that the known has never revealed what we're after, we allow ourselves to look in a different direction – and relax into the unknown. If it takes courage, then it takes courage.

When we step outside our habitual and conditioned ways of being, by *seeing* without the mind's preference or partiality, we allow for ignorance to be dispelled. This seeing *is* the light of awareness that coaxes untruth out of the darkness, allowing us to see it for what it is – simply concepts believed to be true that determined our activities. It's important to notice that we can't *decide* or *make* wisdom bloom; we can only let wisdom bloom. We let it bloom by uncovering the false.

All that's asked of you is to look in the directions you're being pointed – and not just one time. Look until you *see*, knowing the false cannot stand up to close examination. So many have already examined and discovered – and they didn't die. Granted, many have experienced varying degrees of reluctance, fear and trepidation, but so what. If that's what must be experienced, then so be it. It's all just energy anyway – and illusory, so it can't harm or touch what you really are. Nothing can – so don't let what's unreal stop you.

Lastly, you'll find certain words and phrases repeated throughout the book. I ask that you excuse and look beyond any redundancies. In the Zen tradition, this repetitive method is sometimes used in an attempt to wear down the mind in order to go beyond the mind – and realize you're already beyond the mind. This is not the intent here.

Nonetheless, there's a fresh and brand new opportunity to find out what's really true – even in any apparent redundancy you may encounter. Since Truth is singular – and if it's Truth we're really after, pointing to the same changeless essence is requisite. Since there's no wisdom without truth, both are intertwined, forever arising in unison.

Chapter 1
Freedom Beyond Belief

"The word 'belief' is a difficult thing for me. I don't believe. I must have a reason for a certain hypothesis. Either I know a thing, and then I know it – I don't need to believe it."

~ Carl Jung

Any book on wisdom wouldn't be complete if belief wasn't discussed. In fact, if you ever come across a book about wisdom and the topic of belief isn't included, put it down - or just know it's incomplete. It's like ordering cherry pie only to find it didn't come with cherries when you went to eat it. Almost everything we say, think, feel and do is based on belief – or more accurately, our belief system. Strangely enough, we rarely ever look at this mental construct, this thing that governs and dictates so much of our existence. If we're really and truly interested in truth, it is essential that we look at what belief really is, and how it stacks up to truth.

Webster defines belief as *"A state or habit of mind in which trust or confidence is placed in some person or thing. Belief is the mental act, condition or habit of placing trust or confidence in a person or thing, a mental acceptance or conviction in the truth or actuality of something; to believe is to accept with veracity."* I prefer to define belief as "unquestioned acceptance of something in the absence of reason; unquestioned acceptance of an alleged fact without positive knowledge or proof." We say, "I believe in God; I believe that people should be kind to animals and the elderly; I believe that blue is a more soothing color than green, and I believe that the Republicans have a better plan to revitalize the economy than the Democrats."

And? None of it really means anything, intrinsically anyway. But it does dictate our experience. The fact is, on this planet right now of almost seven billion people, there are literally millions upon millions of differing beliefs swirling around in people's heads. There's nothing inherently wrong with belief, but how easy do you think it is to find agreement among beliefs? How easy do you think it is to engender the kind of mutual respect for another, even when beliefs are diametrically opposed? When someone says to you, "We have polar opposite worldviews," what are they really saying to you? *Hey, I really like the way you think; let's get together real soon!* I highly doubt it. They're not trying to bond or connect with you, are they? They're not conveying a sense of respect or appreciation for *your* perspective, are they? In their mind, belief is enough to establish "truth" or knowing.

Identified with mind, it's no wonder this happens. However, truth isn't found *in* the mind, and truth certainly won't ever be realized by looking *with* the mind. It's certainly never found in the writings of any book – this one included – no matter how highly regarded that book is. Your perspective may come from seeing what's actually real and true, but they won't be able to see or understand that as long as they maintain belief is enough to establish what's true. If your perspective is truly one of realization that comes from the heart wisdom that already knows – and not from a belief that's manufactured and held onto in the mind, you won't be bothered one bit.

Why would you need to defend what you *know* is true? Those who believe do this; they defend their beliefs. They tend to argue back and forth (often in a very subtle way) trying to convince the other that their belief is the right one. Let's be honest: How can we be objective when we've got so much invested in our belief? We can't. And there are those that vehemently defend what they think they "know." It's a valid indicator that they're operating from belief. It's not a bad or wrong thing, but it's incumbent upon us to know when we really don't know. They say, "You just gotta believe!" No, actually I don't. In fact, if I don't know, I don't need to deceive myself and believe that I know. I don't need to create a belief in order to feel in control.

Nevertheless, beliefs can serve as a bridge, but ultimately the bridge must collapse, leaving you hanging on for dear life. Because the bridge wasn't constructed with the proper materials, it wasn't designed to support over time. If a belief gets created spontaneously, without my intent, I can see through it – and discard it. But first, in order to see through it, I need to notice what my experience is as a result of that belief. I can peacefully rest in not knowing – and in that allowance of not knowing, and only until then, the known can reveal itself. If everything you presently "know" and believe in your mind still hasn't revealed the pot of gold (whatever that is for you) at the end of the rainbow, then doesn't it follow that the unknown is where your "answer" lies?

Millions of people have been slaughtered in the name of God and religion, practiced from belief –

in wars, inquisitions, political uprisings, revolts, ethnic "cleansings" and the like. Unless our consciousness is significantly raised, we are destined to repeat the same behaviors. We pay the ultimate price for such ignorance, becoming more desensitized to the true value of human life. More importantly, we remain in the dark to our true identity. Despite most acting as if truth and belief is the same thing, they are not. In fact, they are very different. Even if a revered and highly respected person believes in something – even has his own national television or radio show with a large following, it makes no difference.

Being lulled into a false sense of security (because you share the same beliefs as a person of "authority" or large group of people, however distinguished) doesn't validate your belief. Your security is rooted in an illusory story – and not what's actual. If it doesn't agree with actual evidence, there's no validity in the real world. At one time, highly intelligent and respected men accepted as scientific FACT, that the world was flat, and the sun revolved around the earth. Belief and faith doesn't establish truth or fact, regardless of how many people believe, or for how long they've believed it. Why do we pretend they're the same? Fear usually – and the potential discomfort we'll feel when our beliefs are exposed as falsehoods.

Please don't misunderstand me. This isn't about bashing beliefs. I'm not suggesting beliefs are to be avoided by any stretch. Nor am I implying that you shouldn't have them, so please don't infer that, either. How silly I'd be to suggest resisting what gets formed within us, naturally and spontaneously. In many cases, beliefs are functional and even necessary. For instance, most of us believe that it's a really good idea not to drive 100 mph if we don't want to pay for a speeding ticket. Most of us believe that in order to be successful at anything in life, we must put in the time and effort needed to accomplish whatever it is that we want.

Most of us believe that staying clear of the edge of a cliff with a five hundred foot canyon drop below is good for our physical safety and survival. Most of us believe that eating healthy and exercising is very beneficial to our overall health and wellbeing. And yet, when it comes to the more meaningful and important aspects of our lives, like realizing truth, enjoying the relationship with our selves and others, we tend to rely on belief. We've been taught to. Belief certainly has the ability to soothe and comfort for a while, but ultimately, like a house of cards, it must collapse. Beliefs almost always fall short – because they must. If it's truth we are after, we don't have the luxury of belief.

With belief comes doubt; it's just the way it works. Belief and doubt reside on two sides of the same restless coin. Neither is the "bad guy," and neither is to be resisted. Seen through, yes, but never resisted. Wisdom sees that what we oppose, we only strengthen. Many beliefs are survival based – and good for us. Like I *believe* that if I go skiing down the expert level diamond trail on the slopes, I'm most likely going to wipe out; I might even get seriously injured or killed. If I'm standing under a large oak tree in a lightning storm, I believe that I better find safer shelter, and quick. But when it comes to the bigger issues that require introspection and contemplation, belief has little ultimate value.

Faced with anything, I either presently know, or I don't know. Since I don't need to engage in self-deception, I don't need to rely on belief. Since I am willing not to know, belief doesn't get created to serve as a go-between. Generally, beliefs don't unite. Beliefs are divisive when we insist that our beliefs represent truth, but yours don't. This divisiveness can cause bloodshed – lots of it. Have you noticed once you believe in something, you generally stop thinking about it? You stop examining whether that thing you believe in is actually true or not. And that's okay, unless it's a belief that determines the quality of your existence, or how you meet each moment.

The majority of us approach the big questions in life by constructing a set of ideas and beliefs in our minds – or taking on what others "of authority" tell us about those bigger issues. We end up depending on them to tell us how life really is, instead of relying on our actual and lived experience to tell us what's really so.   As you may have noticed, these explanations often end up being about as useful as a table with three legs.   They just don't hold up. Because of their inherent instability, they must topple over.   They ultimately fail to provide us the security we seek, because they *can't ever* provide the security we seek.   If we look to belief to provide us lasting security, we're looking in the wrong direction.

Instead of seeing that beliefs don't ultimately deliver what we seek, what do we typically do? We go shopping! We go shopping for, say, another table, but this time, one with four legs and a higher quality wood like mahogany. We reason that surely, four higher quality legs (a new and "better" belief) must be more stable than three legs! For a while, this new table supports us, and we even invite others to sit at our table and experience it for themselves. They may like our table until it, too, must topple over – sometimes with our guests at the table.   It can get kind of messy sometimes!

So, this works for a time, and temporarily provides us a false sense of security and comfort, until it doesn't anymore.   Invariably, at different stages in our lives, if we are conscious, many of us discover that when it comes to our human affairs, beliefs are inherently unstable by nature. We see that if we deal in the realm of belief, uncertainty must eventually follow. With belief comes insecurity. This is the nature of belief, like a scorpion's nature is to sting. We see this by the pain or discomfort we experience as a direct result of believing in a particular thing when it doesn't hold up. Some beliefs are very comforting, and can be for a long time. Thus, we get duped into thinking they can be relied upon permanently. Since everything is in a constant state of change and flow, beliefs can't ever capture what changes.

When we look closely, we notice that beliefs get spontaneously created in our minds, so we can make sense of the world around us. They get manufactured in our minds so we can navigate our way through life. *Most of the time, we don't consciously create a belief – and yet, we take ownership of it as if we did create it!* If we can see this very important point, we are less likely to identify with belief. Instead of identifying with belief – and then acting from it, we can simply notice it's there – and without judgment or resistance, choose not to act on it. If we're really willing to acknowledge what's actual, our awareness of it often disarms and dissolves it.

The truth is, without beliefs, most of us would feel vulnerable and insecure. There's nothing wrong or bad about this. However, when it comes to the bigger issues in life, beliefs are very limited and self-fulfilling. We see what we believe, and we believe what we see – and so our life goes. However, before beliefs are created, there is an opportunity to see what's real and actual. All we must do is just look and *see* for ourselves what's actual, instead of assuming our belief is adequate, or representative of what's actual. The false cannot stand up to close examination. It's not meant to. If the false cannot stand up to examination, why would we ever NOT examine our beliefs that ultimately determine our experience? Either indifference or false evidence appearing real – fear.

Children believe pretty much everything their parents tell them. Since most parents neglect to teach their children the difference between "bad behavior" and the goodness that they intrinsically *always* are, it's no wonder we have such problems with low self-esteem. Being reprimanded as often as they are, most children grow up believing they *are* their behavior. And so, there's a big difference between having our child believe that eating yellow snow is bad, or walking on thin ice isn't such a great idea, and having that same child believe he or she *is* their behavior. Thus, when he or she acts out, they *believe* they are a bad person.

Sure, it is wise to avoid eating yellow snow and walking on thin ice, but deeper wisdom sees the greater importance of teaching our children the significant difference between his or her behaviors, and who they are as humans. If we want our children to love themselves as they are – and become productive members of society, we're responsible to teach them this essential distinction.

As small children, we are encouraged to believe in things like the Easter Bunny, Santa Claus and the Tooth Fairy. Seemingly innocuous, this conditioning invariably sets the tone and creates the mold for the way the child sees life. Parents who teach their children to believe without questioning, ultimately programs that child to turn to belief as something to rely on – the kind of reliance that just accepts on faith, without any examination.

After all, you better not pout, you better not shout, you better not cry, I'm telling you why ... Santa Claus is coming to town. He sees you when you're sleeping, he knows when you're awake; he knows if *you've* been "bad" or "good," so be good for goodness sake! The fat guy in the red suit and the long white beard is watching YOU, so if you want him sliding down your chimney, *you* better behave. If not, you'll wake up Christmas morning to find coal in your stockings! Innocent and harmless, eh? By the way, don't forget to leave him cookies and milk.

We have very little recognition of just how much our minds play in fantasyland. We won't ever get this recognition from reading a book, or listening to what other "reputable" sources say about it. Actually, there is nothing to "get." You already possess that which you seek – if you would just see it. How can we *get* what we are? Before we grasp onto any concept that tries to explain things, see what's being seen in your direct experience, already. It has

11

absolutely nothing to do with belief. As humans, we have a remarkable ability to make things up, and pretend as if they're so. Fantasy, driven by imagination, gives us the ability to enjoy pleasurable experiences; we could say it's a functional necessity in order for the mind to escape what is. Fantasies and imagination require no belief in them in order to enjoy them.

That's the whole point; no belief is needed for us to escape, create and play in our minds. But when we start to believe in our fantasies, or worse... have faith in them, we usually set ourselves up for disappointment, or worse, devastating results. The tragic events that unfolded on September 11, 2001 are, in fact, a direct manifestation of having complete faith in religious belief. Promise of a pleasant afterlife was the reward for those that murdered the infidels, those against the will of Allah. And many volunteered for the cause. Sadly, we aren't even aware we're just killing our Self.

Generally, beliefs don't lead to the real wisdom that transforms a life. How can something un-questioned and accepted on "faith," in the absence of positive knowledge and proof, accomplish this? How can it be the right tool for the job? It's like expecting your four year-old to safely drive you home after you've become too sick to drive. It's not going to happen. We read or hear about the limitations, dangers and monstrous atrocities perpetrated due to opposing beliefs. We're mostly aware that our belief system determines our experience, but for some reason, most of us go about our lives in the same habitual ways, never really stopping to question. Since the tragic stuff doesn't hit home for most of us (it's happening to "others") our personal beliefs usually don't register as something urgent we really need to challenge and re-examine. Our minds entertain and believe in a whole host and variety of things that have nothing to do with truth or reality. Nevertheless, we continue on with the same formula, somehow expecting a different or better result. And life passes by, decades at a time.

What about religion or faith? The word (or concept) "religion" stems from *religio,* which meant, "to bind back very strongly to truth." Interestingly, every religion known to man – and every religion created BY man, was designed to be based in truth, but in actuality, is practiced *from* belief. Thus, it is approached *from* and *by* belief. And yet if you ask most people, they will say that their religion is "true," and that the precepts or scripture they follow are based in truth. Thus, at the core of religion is the promise and opportunity to *see* and experience truth. It isn't about collecting a variety of notions and beliefs *about* truth.

Religion, in and of itself, is not the problem. The confusion immediately arises when we approach religion from belief. Religion is commonly thought to be about belief – and consequently, it's almost always practiced from belief. Its chief concern is actually with knowledge, with knowing. Like religion, science is about getting to the truth of the matter at hand. The word *science* derives from the Latin *scire*, "to know." Science is about knowing, and not about believing. Science goes to extraordinary lengths to test it's beliefs – or what it terms, "hypotheses."

If science cannot prove the validity of a particular hypothesis after comprehensive testing, it's either thrown out or reformulated and tested further. Additionally, conclusions then must be tested by various independent sources to prove its validity. It's a very precise, unbiased and agenda-free method for arriving at truth; it's a method where man's thinking is totally removed from the process. While science is commonly thought to be about real and actual knowledge – and prides itself on not being dependent on belief, it is inevitably very dependent on it. Like fish need water, science needs belief in order to survive.

In fact, without it, it can't function, nor could scientific principles be applied in the discovery of what's out what's scientifically factual. In order for science to function, scientists must dissect the world in order to examine it. It requires that we create and construct versions of the world we experience based upon concepts. And while concepts can never capture or comprehend reality, conceptual models are necessary to come to what's really so. Thus, belief lends itself more valuably to science – and is far more dependent upon it than religion ever is, or needs to be. Conversely, for religion to be of real value to us, it needn't require belief.

"In science it often happens that scientists say, 'You know, that's a really good argument; my position is mistaken,' and they would actually change their minds and you never hear that old view from them again. They really do it. It doesn't happen as often as it should, because scientists are human and change is sometimes painful. But it happens everyday. I cannot recall the last time something like that happened in politics or religion." **Carl Sagan**

However, for centuries, all religions continue to depend on belief – and as a result, people run in all sorts of different directions, insisting their beliefs are "true," while the others are grossly mistaken. All the while, truth non-judgmentally rests quietly, watching the grand delusion go on. Consequently, we see religions at war with each other, each insisting that the other is "wrong" and "immoral." Religion fights science, too. It will claim science's findings can't be true because it doesn't jive with its dogma, its conceptual model of reality.

When faced with – or holding in their hands the reality of dinosaur fossils, and fossils of prehistoric man over a 1.5 million years old (Turkana Boy), one who believes in creationism will either say the bones are fake, or the age of the bones is mistaken. If they *are* real, they must be less than ten thousand years old. French philosopher Frantz Fanon aptly said, *"Sometimes people hold a core belief that is very strong. When they are presented with evidence that works against that belief, the new evidence cannot be accepted. It would create a feeling that is extremely uncomfortable, called cognitive dissonance. And because it is so important to protect the core belief, they will rationalize, ignore and even deny anything that doesn't fit in with their core belief."*

When we rely on Holy Scripture, Sacred Books, Sutra or any other conceptual source or "authority," we are essentially telling ourselves that, in and of ourselves, we cannot or will not arrive at truth. In other words, we unconsciously conclude we don't have the innate capacity to *see* what's actual. We conclude that we need to rely on belief, and/or rely on what someone else said, believed or witnessed. It's all hearsay. In doing so, we give up responsibility to find out for ourselves. Hence, we approach truth or reality from belief – and *believe* it's the right tool for the job. We tell ourselves that we can never truly discern truth from falsehood, or that it's for the special or chosen few.

We reject the very notion that every day common folk like us possess this ability, and that it's reserved for the monks or enlightened found in the caves and monasteries. We may even conclude that the enlightened and free are simply operating from belief, too – and that they're just more convincing! What's most interesting is that those who say this rarely ever do the inner work themselves. Those who say this rarely investigate and question all of it before jumping to hasty, unfounded conclusions rooted in belief.

If religion is fundamentally concerned with direct knowledge of truth, those that practice religion must see that belief isn't the thing that will assist them arriving at truth. We need to see that in order to really wake up to who we really are – and arrive at the truth – *and let wisdom bloom* – we must go beyond the mental constructs of belief, to the heart wisdom that already knows. That is, we need to arrive at where we already are, the space that is prior to mental creations – the awareness that encompasses all mental constructions – the awareness that radiates from the heart. Only when we stop leaving will we arrive.

All that's simply needed is to *see* what's already being seen. This may sound abstract, like a mystery wrapped within a riddle, but it's anything but. It's right here, in plain view. We just don't see it. Science can't actually reveal to us the real nature of ultimate truth. Instead, this is the ultimate role and responsibility of religion. Religion doesn't have in its operating manual ways to test and validate hypothesis, nor should it. It doesn't need, nor should it make use of, hypothesis and belief of any kind.

Provided that religion doesn't rely heavily on belief in order to arrive at truth, religion can be of real value.

Those that continue to identify with the mind's natural tendency to grasp onto something are much more inclined to say, "Yes, that's it – that's the truth and I believe it!" They don't yet *see* that truth isn't something we *can* grasp onto or believe in. In fact, ultimate reality or truth, being beyond belief or anything the mind can conceptually construct, isn't something that *can* be approached with belief or concepts. Although we try in vain, we literally cannot conceptually arrive at truth in any way, shape or form. We interpret those times, when our beliefs bring about an energetic feeling of truth in the body to *be* the real thing.

We conclude that since our belief *feels* true, then it must *be* true. Until we cannot see or sense any other way, we will continue to cling to our beliefs *about* reality, never realizing that they're simply fabrications that function as alleviating go-betweens. In our need to make sense of the world, we will cling to our conceptual models about reality, and therefore, never experience reality immediately and directly. Our need to control and feel comforted by our concepts will continue to overshadow our willingness to not know.

The paradoxical irony is that, it is only in our complete and absolute willingness NOT to know, can truth reveal itself as that which never left us in the first place. At some point, we must get in touch with our most fundamental impulse, the impulse to be free – free from our minds and free from our emotions. We just want to be okay with whatever arises. If the mind races and our emotions go on a rollercoaster ride, we want to be okay with that. The thing to *see* is, that whenever we ARE absolutely okay with the contents of our minds – and if we are absolutely okay with whatever emotions arise, both the mind and emotions settle down. Don't believe me; check it out for yourself. Resist the temptation to draw a conclusion that says you'd be in resignation mode, or that if you don't resist, you'll get more what you don't want. Neither is true.

This impulse to be free is expressed so beautifully in the numerous religions throughout the world. This impulse points to the open, innocent and pure heart and mind that embraces all, without any distinction or preference. It is a lover of what is – not a lover of what could or should be. Your true nature loves without condition or preference; it is a lover with eternal loyalty. Whenever we're able to retreat from the busyness of life and quiet our minds, we get an immediate and direct sense of this reality that we already are.

Unfortunately, in our fascination with the countless objects in our field of perception vying for our attention, our minds are rarely quiet. As a result, most aren't in touch with this inner impulse to be free. The truth is, that if this impulse were really looked into, it would liberate us. This impulse requires us to look within, to take our habitual focus off objects "out there" – and look at how things really are, not how we think or wish them to be. We often read these pointers, but we often gloss over them without investigating them. Belief in separation is the original sin – and every problem we have stems from this misunderstanding.

Adam believed he was separate from that which he sought – and this misperception has trickled down throughout the ages. We still believe we are separate from the truth – that there's truth, god, reality *and* us. This is the crux of our problem. The chief aim of spirituality – and religion for that matter, is to settle down, return home and realize that separation is a complete and utter illusion. *Be Still and Know* – and realize that separation doesn't exist. In fact, unity, not separation, *is* the fundamental essence of the nature of all things seen and unseen. Oneness is the ground of being that everything springs from. As the Ninth-century Chinese Zen teacher Huang Po said, *"The foolish reject what they see, not what they think; the wise reject what they think, not what they see."*

When we get "suckered in" by the mind and its beliefs, we face the direction that typically hurts; we remain confused and unsure. Since we've been taught since birth to believe what we think, this is a very natural thing that happens. How can it not be? Not only do we believe what we think, we take it a step further and conclude we *are what we think;* we let the dominoes fall! Sure, we can believe good and empowering things about ourselves, but what happens if we stop believing those things? What then? If beliefs change, as they often do, aren't we basing our security on something that comes and goes? What happens when others refute what we believe about ourselves? What happens when life and circumstance display something completely different than our beliefs about them?

Modifying or strengthening our beliefs is a band-aid approach. Questioning their validity is a rooting out approach. Fortunately, we are wired in such a way that illusion doesn't feel so good. If we weren't, we'd probably never wake up to what we are, and see beyond the limitations of belief to what's true. Fortunately, we are wired with the capacity to realize what's true, too. Are YOU your beliefs, or do you have beliefs? If you can notice the beliefs your mind entertains and clings to, how could you actually *be* those beliefs? If you can notice the actual for-mation of a particular belief, wouldn't YOU have to be fundamentally prior to that formation?

You sure would. If you keep looking, this alone could be the pointer that leads to awakening. Seriously. And it's not the mind that notices. Wisdom sees that we are not our beliefs. It knows that instead, we have beliefs. Wisdom sees that when we aren't feeling quite right, we must not be in harmony with life and the laws or principles of our own experience. As long as we're breathing, we continue to receive clues and indicators all the time. Wisdom blooms when we rest in the awareness that is prior to the formation of, and subsequent belief in, our beliefs. *Any time we aren't feeling quite right, we can be sure it is an indicator that we aren't in harmony with what's actual and true.*

Any time we aren't feeling quite right, we know we hopped on the train of thought and belief and went for a ride. Isn't this feedback fortunate? As I stated in my first book, "Born To Be Happy – How to Uncover Your Natural State of Happiness," the only time we ever really suffer is when we believe whatever is actually occurring, shouldn't be occurring. Since minds don't deal in simplicity, it overlooks this simple and transcending truth. Yes, that supercomputer you possess has real difficulty in simplicity. Pretty ironic, wouldn't you say? When we resist what is actually happening in any moment, we believe that something else "should" be happening. Is this ever true? No, it isn't. But since we believe it, we must suffer.

So what do we do when our conceptual models of reality don't ultimately support us? What can we do with the resulting confusion that must inevitably arise from belief? If we can't look to our beliefs to make sense of our world and comfort us long term, where do we turn to provide us that comfort and security? Instead of depending on our mental constructs (that have no substance or reality because they're literally made up and sustained by our minds) we can look in a different direction.

This "direction" is our actual experience in the moment, prior to belief, and prior to concepts. And that is to just *see* what's happening without labeling it. We must confirm in our own experience what's real and true, without relying on an outside source. Before we label something as "good" or "bad" or "right" or "wrong," we can just be with what is, with equanimity and neutrality – without any preference or bias. Wisdom sees that, in some instances, beliefs can appropriately serve as a temporary bridge to carry us across to the other side, the side of stability and clarity.

Like surrender, *seeing* takes no effort at all. If you think it takes a lot of effort and struggle, think again. Fear (false evidence appearing real) is typically the main obstacle. But when you see this "energy of emotion" is simply a result of erroneous thinking, temporary fear won't stop you. It's just a reminder we're not in harmony, that's all. Why make it any bigger than it is? We must be willing not to have it our way, and not to have it conform to how we think it *should* be, which is just more belief. Most of us *believe* that not knowing isn't a good thing, and something to be avoided altogether, because it must bring insecurity and vulnerability.

This is just another unquestioned belief assumed to be true. We habitually stop short of asking, "Is this really true?" When we stop short of asking whether something is true or not, obviously we aren't going to investigate our experience to confirm whether it's true or not! Why do we insist on relying on belief when we're capable of finding out what is actually so in our direct experience? If we can't discover what is actual, why must we create a belief? What's it like not to know? Isn't it spacious and peaceful when the mind doesn't get involved? Check it out.

If we want to live from our natural state of wisdom – and if we want to be in harmony with life in an intimate and transforming way, we recognize that two of our best friends are vigilance and discernment. We must recognize and discern what beliefs bring us pain, and be vigilant when they operate in our experience. Examining our beliefs is essential if we seek greater wisdom and happiness. The reality is, each and every belief held can be directly refuted by countless others. Doesn't this speak to the validity of belief? Truth is eternal and changeless – and can't ever be successfully refuted, no matter how eloquent or seemingly logical the argument.

In a moment of real clarity, we can see that, instead of placing our faith in our beliefs, opinions, past conditioning and anything else that comes from our minds, we can place our trust in our direct experience. That is, our actual experience prior to any concepts, thoughts about, judgments, resistances, desires, expectations and preferences. We place our trust in our being that already meets the moment as it is, and not as our minds want or prefer it to be. And we notice our experience.

Only when we are willing to drop all of our notions, assumptions and opinions about what we think we know in any moment, do we give ourselves the opportunity to really *see what's actual versus what's illusory.* If it's already happening, it can't be any other way. This one thing realized, can change the entire world. The mind will try to convince us, that indeed, something *else* should or could be happening. And since most are identified with the mind, it's natural most believe the dictates of the mind! As the mind goes, we go.

In its infinite wisdom, it will tell us that something else can, should or could be happening – you know, because it "knows" best. But, it's *never* true. If it's already happening, why don't we see that it can't be any other way than it is? Why do we have such trouble seeing that this is the crux of our suffering? *Never* in any moment of anyone's existence has anything happened that shouldn't have happened. I realize some will have a huge problem with this statement, but nonetheless, it's true. The fact that your mind may believe otherwise changes nothing. *See* this and be free.

Once the barriers of ignorance are identified and seen through – and you refrain from replacing them with "new and improved beliefs," or buying into new ones that get spontaneously created, you find yourself living in the flow of life. Wholly unconcerned, yet intimately engaged, something of a higher order guides your activities. Fear and doubt leave your system, and you move when life moves you to move. And it's never conceptual; it's always experiential. That's when you know. And when you don't know, you look until you *see*. And if you still don't see, you rest in the knowing that, apparently, you aren't yet meant to see. You'll *see* when you *see*.

Doubts may come and go. But your own natural self, the one for whom the doubts appear is present and clear, and not subject to any of the doubts. That fact of being, which is the ground of the doubts, is the doubt-free reality. The awareness of doubt isn't in doubt at all. *Seeing* this, you effortlessly exit from of any possible doubts raised by the mind – because you *see* what's true. The mind may continue to have its doubts, but your being is present, beyond any and all doubt. Freedom is beyond belief. Do you need a belief to BE what you are? Know this by confirming it for yourself. When you truly allow yourself not to know, and when you let your actual experience blossom, wisdom blooms.

Chapter 2
Dead On Arrival

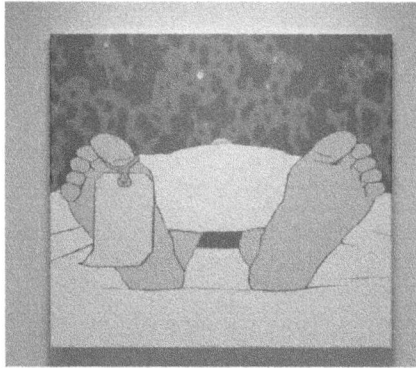

"Surely the memory of an event cannot pass for the event itself. Nor can the anticipation. There is something exceptional, unique, about the present event, which the previous, or the coming, do not have. There is a livingness about it – an actuality; it stands out as the illumined. There is the 'stamp of reality' on the actual, which the past and future do not have."

~ Nisargadatta Maharaj

No doubt you're well aware that human beings are wired to gain pleasure and avoid pain. More intimately, being human, you experience this tendency almost all the time, don't you? Just because we are hooked up this way doesn't mean that we have to live from this inclination, does it? In other words, must we live out our lives this way, especially *if we see* that avoidance for what we don't want and grasping after what we do want is a consistent recipe for experiencing the constant ups and downs of life? Fortunately, we sure don't.

Instead, we can welcome what comes our way, knowing that everything is in flux and that nothing remains – and see where that leads us. We always have the option to go back to our old way of being, right? You don't have to be highly intelligent (I'm not) and you certainly don't have to be special. None of us are – sorry to break it to you! You do, however, have to possess the earnest desire to be willing to look and see for yourself how your experience has a strong tendency to be pleasant when things go right and unpleasant when they don't.

In order to transcend this human mind's impulse to "avoid and grasp", we must look at what might happen if we simply welcome whatever shows up in our experience. While we don't have to be the sharpest tools in the shed, we do, however, have to be very observant – and without any agenda, willing to see what's actual. As long as our focus is on avoiding pain and gaining pleasure, we will always be subject to suffering at some point. By resisting what is (and placing our energy towards avoiding pain and gaining pleasure) we invite pain and potential suffering, only every time. It is consistent, reliable and predictable.

In the human experience, have you noticed that pain is inevitable and suffering is optional and unnecessary? When I first heard this many years ago, I got real curious and I had to know how and why this was so. Hearing that suffering was optional really intrigued me. I later discovered that *being human, we will never be free from pain, but there is a way to be free from suffering.* Those who don't feel any pain in this life aren't really engaged and fully present to their actual experience.

Enlightenment or liberation doesn't mean one is free from pain. It doesn't mean that we rest in bliss all the time, living beyond what the "unenlightened" experience. This is a myth that abounds in many spiritual circles, and isn't very useful. Enlightenment simply means to see things as they are, prior to thought or belief. If anything, even the most enlightened among us experience pain in some form or another, whether it's from the loss of a loved one or something else.

The difference is that those who are awake and free know that pain is part of the package of being human, so no resistance is offered to what arises; they allow pain to pass through as it's literally just the next experience consciousness is having.

Now granted, *seeing* this, so much untruth drops away, never to clamor for our attention anymore. Allowing any moment to be as it is makes for an even richer experience for the one who doesn't reject. It is *this* allowing that keeps suffering away, because the awakened know that resistance *to* pain is what causes suffering. Awake and free beings don't work against themselves. They know that whenever they are willing to have *any* experience, they are truly conscious, and therefore, free from suffering.

The nice thing is, when you really see how your experience unfolds, this allowing and welcoming begins to happen spontaneously and naturally. You don't have to consciously decide to welcome and allow. When you discern truth from falsehood, you find yourself living more spontaneously and non-judgmentally. There is an energetic movement that just happens on its own, without any conscious choice involved – *because* you finally saw what's true.

Old habit patterns that once hurt and divide are dissolved. Simply put, whenever we are willing to have *any* experience we are conscious, and therefore, free from suffering. Suffering happens when we unconsciously resist what's actually happening. What's happening is called reality.

What you think or believe about reality is just that – just what you think or believe about it. Do our labels, judgments and definitions about reality *change* reality, or does it change our perception, and therefore, experience *of* reality? We can't change reality for reality never changes; we can only change our perception of it. What does change is everything that comes and goes in reality, like our thoughts, feelings, experiences, etc. Being in alignment with reality enables us to live in harmony with it. Consequently, we don't suffer because we're no longer in opposition to it. This simple truth escapes most of us, when in fact, it's right here, unhidden and in plain view for us to *see*.

When we believe that any experience we are presently happening shouldn't be happening, we invite and create more friction – and we actually hold in place what we *don't* want. We somehow go unconscious and allow ourselves to be deluded in thinking resistance is a good strategy to get what we really want.

Alternatively, when we know that any experience we are having is the only way it can be happening in *that* moment, we consciously allow for another possibility to arise in the next moment. If we really desire to have a different reality than the one we are presently having, we give up the battle. We no longer feed what we don't want with wishing it

32

were different than it is. In this way, we just removed any energy that would continue to feed it and give it life. When there's no energy that goes into it, it can't continue to survive.

In this way, we don't unconsciously torment and confuse ourselves because the negative energy that feeds what we don't want isn't present anymore. Aside from a masochist, who would consciously choose to self-torment? Any experience we are having is *never* the problem. It is what we tell ourselves *about* the experience we are having that's the problem. Roman slave and Philosopher, Epictetus conveyed this a few thousand years ago. Having a negative, pushing-away orientation towards any experience we are having must become divisive and painful. It is the secondary interpretation, an overlay we place upon what's happening that disturbs us, and not the actual event or happening.

Look and see if this is true for you – and don't believe a word you read here. Literally everything is energy with a distinct vibration to it – and inherent in every thought, belief, word spoken and action taken has a vibration. That distinct and corollary vibration determines our state of being, and how much ease or strife we experience. Every intention we have, and every intention that we evoke, carries with it a certain vibration that either leads to an expansion or contraction of our being. Our bodies are indeed sensing instruments of the divine, feeling and expressing directly from the level of consciousness it sprang from.

Wisdom sees we are wise to live from this realization and notice *what* are bodies are telling us. Wisdom blooms when we actually live in accord with that feedback. When we meet what is actually occurring with neutrality, acceptance, and even *gratitude*, we work with ourselves, not against ourselves. Gratitude arises when we see the truth of opposites. Once we REALLY SEE that we literally cannot experience joy, unless pain is also a potential experience, we have a much less tendency to react with resistance. After all, we all prefer less pain and more happiness, don't we? While I don't resist negative or unpleasant experiences, like most humans, I prefer pleasant ones - but I'm okay with unpleasant ones.

We see that joy and pain are two sides of the same coin; these opposite experiences are a functional necessity. Without them, we couldn't experience *anything*. In my book, *"The Dance of Imperfection - Living in Perfect Harmony with Life,"* I go into this in much more detail. When we see that to resist what's *already* happening only binds us to what we *don't* want, we untie ourselves from the bondage we never wanted in the first place. No longer are we shackled, because we know how it works in our experience. As the saying goes, what we resist persists, and what we focus on expands and grows stronger.

Argue with reality and suffer every time. We stop the battle and just intend for something else, while being okay with what's already arising in our experience. It's a recipe we can count on to deliver the ease of being desired. We have a wide variety of notions and beliefs about what freedom and truth is. We seldom *see* that it is these notions and beliefs that further distort and muddy our freedom, and in fact, keep us confused and contracted. What we say, think and believe about freedom can never lead us to freedom itself, because Truth and Reality can never be approached through these means. Reality and freedom can never be what we *think* it is. Reality and Freedom can never be what we believe, say or read that it is; it's always prior, underneath and all encompassing.

When we insist on our ideas and beliefs as being accurate representations for what is true and real, we only create more bondage for ourselves. It is well worth repeating because this truth is so powerful, liberating and transformational: the word or concept, being a descriptor and a symbol, is never the actual. Babies have no idea what words mean when they come out of the womb. We all know it takes years to learn the various labels for existence, and then to put them together into a storyline. Words have no intrinsic meaning. Words and concepts, being inherently limited, can only point to Truth or Freedom.

As it says in The Tao, *"The Tao that can be spoken is not the eternal Tao"* and *"The name than can be named is not the eternal name."* It can only be pointed to with language made of concepts – and language, being finite descriptions "about" things is inherently limiting and dualistic. Truth, being infinite, is ONE – and has only ever been ONE. It's not an object, despite our repeated attempts to make it one. And since it encompasses and precedes ALL (including your mind) it can never be adequately described or understood with the mind.

And yet, we actually think and believe we can accurately describe the Infinite Source of Everything, God or whatever you like to call it. It is beyond name and form. It makes perfect sense that there is a direct relationship between being more conscious and experiencing less inner division and suffering. We just can't feel good if we are divided inside. Inner division is painful, mostly because it's source is illusion. Naturally, the less conscious we are, the more we are divided; the more divided we are, the more we suffer. Rising above our conditioning (while including it) is needed if we want to express and enjoy are authentic selves.

Aren't we really here to enjoy and express who we really are? I sure am. If we want to transcend the collective consciousness that mostly deals in belief and separation – and the consequential perception of scarcity, competition and fear, we must see through illusion to what's true. If we want to transcend the inevitable experience of fleeting happiness that stems from making our happiness dependent on outside factors, we need to see through unreality to reality. Therefore, we are called to *transcend and include*, not transcend and resist. In fact, we can only transcend *when* we include all of it.

If it's more joy and freedom we want, we don't really have the luxury to say, "I want this experience all day, but I be damned if I have time for that crappy experience!" Instead, we must include all of it, the pleasurable and the un-pleasurable – but only if we want to truly enjoy our lives in way that's rooted in truth and reality. What we don't understand, we usually dismiss as pure folly, don't we? Isn't that human nature? So, if that is your reaction to the following statement, I invite you to reconsider. *What is happening in any moment is exactly what should be happening; what is happening in any moment is meant to be happening.*

The truth is, any other conclusion that we come to is insane. Why? First of all, can you prove that your assessment is absolutely true, that whatever is happening shouldn't actually be happening? In other words, can you prove that something else should or could be happening? If you're annoyed, just notice and welcome that, too. It is all appropriate and okay. Isn't it insane to resist reality, or what is? Secondly, check out your experience when you want your present experience to be other than it actually is. It never feels quite right, does it? In fact, it can be very painful.

It's simple, yet despite our actual experience of contraction and dis-ease felt in the body (that results from believing anything can be different than it is in *that* moment) we make it complex by believing what our minds tell us. We say that whatever is happening shouldn't be happening – and that something else *could* or *should* be happening. In and through every breath you've ever taken, in and through each heartbeat, and during each and every moment of your existence, no matter what you've gone through, it's never been true.

For anything to be true, it must be 100% true, not 99% true. If it's 99.9% true, it isn't true. We call things "true" that don't even come close to true, and we often call things that are mostly true, true. Sure, things can be relatively true, but not ultimately (or absolutely) true. But let's call a spade a spade, okay? If it isn't 100% true all the time, it isn't really true. It never was true, and it never will be true. Granted, there are thoughts and beliefs that are truer than others, more serving and beneficial than others, but no thoughts and beliefs are ultimately true. We just believe they are. The thought is never the actual – it just serves as a pointer to the actual.

What is true doesn't come and go, either. It must be present all the time in order for it to be true. Beliefs, opinions, judgments and assumptions change all the time, and therefore, come and go. We make them up as we go along, changing or altering them to suit our needs. There's nothing wrong with this, unless we become so invested in them, insisting that they're true. Can you claim without any doubt whatsoever, that in any given moment, something else should or could be happening? Can that be true – can that ever be true? No, it can't ever be true. *Any thought that is contrary and in resistance to what is actually occurring in any moment is false and DOA, dead on arrival.*

Anything we bring from the past is a dead thing that we give life to. Past, being memory only, is a dead thing. The only living reality is right here and right now, this present moment. Because our attention is life giving and supportive, what we give our attention and belief to, lives on and shapes our experience. When we cling to a belief, judgment or opinion that insists it can be different than it is, we essentially give a dead thing (illusion and lies) life. Literally, we put on "life support" that which is dead and unreal to begin with, and bring it into this moment. We prop it up as real – like the dead guy from the movie, "Weekend at Bernie's!"

We resurrect what was already dead, and since it can work for a while (we can fool others like they did in the movie and carry around our propped up, dead illusion) we get tricked into believing it's a solid and lasting formula. Then, we live *from that lie believed in* - and illusion and confusion ensues. Consequently, we can never feel and experience the true contentment that we really desire because our foundation is built on sand, not rock. It's constructed on illusion, and therefore, it won't ever hold up. Wisdom sees that self-deception is painful, while truth telling ultimately isn't.

Since we aren't doing any of this intentionally, compassion knows everything is okay the way it is. The more we see this, the less it will occur in our experience. Therefore, beating ourselves up is the last thing we need to add to the situation. Compassion sees that yes, we constantly dupe ourselves into thinking a thing shouldn't be happening, because quite frankly, we don't want it to be happening! We sure don't mind something is happening if we *want* it to be happening, do we? That may sound very silly, and even painfully obvious. But what's sillier is to resist what's already happening. What's most silly is thinking what's already happening shouldn't be happening!

Wisdom sees how silly this *all* is (some call it the Cosmic Joke) and then compassion steps in, knowing it's just human nature doing it's thing, until it doesn't anymore. When we impartially see this entire cycle being played, we notice its momentum come to a halt. It's like our car coming to a halt because it just ran out of gas. Bringing a certain amount of levity to the situation can act as a dissolving agent, too. Laughter doesn't bind; it disperses and frees. When we look to our minds (and not our direct experience) to tell us what's true and real, we invite more suffering. In fact, absolutely every experience that you've ever had in your entire life could not have gone down any different than it did! See this and be free.

I was both shocked and relieved when I saw the truth of this in my own experience, and not what my mind told me. Seeing the truth of this goes beyond belief, and must be beyond belief. How many times have we come across this kind of statement, shrugging it off without really testing it out? I invite you to see how this is true in your own experience, too. If you do, your life will never be same. That's a promise. Like we said in the first chapter, the aim isn't to rid ourselves of beliefs, opinions and assumptions. That would be ridiculous because many beliefs are a functional necessity.

This isn't a book about bashing beliefs. If you believe it's not a good idea to walk across a congested highway of cars traveling over 65mph, would that be beneficial to your health? Of course it would, as you may be struck and die. But, I am "assuming" that since you are reading this book called, *"When Wisdom Blooms ... Awaken The Sage Within"*, you know this, and are interested in living more from what you know and realize is true – and not what you "believe" is true! Is this a safe assumption? Besides, this isn't so much about the obvious, physical survival stuff, like it's wise to believe swimming in shark-infested waters is bad for you.

"Getting rid" of beliefs, ideas, assumptions and opinions isn't really necessary, nor is it our aim. There is a much more efficient way that takes much less effort, and the effects are long term. Being one who prefers the path of least resistance, this got my full and undivided attention: Just see through these illusory concepts and notions as untruth, and they drop away by themselves. When we really *see* their unreality, they leave our system, usually for good.

Rarely, if ever, are we duped anymore. When we see that the sky really isn't blue, but only appears blue, our belief in a blue sky as actual drops away – yet we can fully appreciate and enjoy the soothing appearance of it being blue. When we see an old, limiting story we've carried around for so long isn't true, it drops away. We don't have to get rid of it; all that's really required is to see through our erroneous belief; it dissolves *in and through* that seeing. To see it as untrue is to let go. It's passive in that we don't need to "do" anything, yet it's effectively powerful.

Now, I am well aware that right now, your mind may be telling you a whole different story about this, so I hope you aren't throwing out the baby with the bathwater. If this is so, please consider suspending your judgment and read on as I will attempt to make this more clear shortly. We've been conditioned to typically think that (if we don't resist an unpleasant, unwanted experience) we won't get what we *do* want, right? "What, just lay down and take it? I'll get more of it then, wont' I?" After all, doesn't this conclusion seem, and even feel, logical?

Besides, haven't we experienced many achievements in the past with this attitude, that when we resist something, we drive it out of our experience? While it may appear this way on the surface, on closer examination, our unconscious strategy doesn't work long term. Further, we think that to allow what is to be as it is, we'd essentially be living in a state of resignation, passively allowing what we *don't* want to be in our experience? We conclude that, like the majority, we must "fight" for what we want – and do whatever it takes if we really want to attain a specific goal, thing or state of being!

Our minds will erroneously conclude that if we don't resist a thing, that it will continue on in our experience. It's as if we feel that our resistance is the fire extinguisher that puts out the fire. In actuality, our resistance is fuel that adds to the fire. We equate an attitude of passively allowing with being a doormat for all to walk on, inviting more unwanted and undesired experiences to come our way. I thought, believed and acted from this perspective for many years. It was only until I considered the possibility that maybe my strategy was counter-productive.

It was only until this strong doubt seeped in, that I saw my approach worked *against* the law of my experience. I saw that when I allowed what was happening *to* happen, as I intended for something else to happen, change occurred. I noticed what I didn't want left my experience rather quickly when I no longer resisted it. It's like I starved it. When I saw that believing the thoughts in my head wasn't the best formula (for peace and happiness) I made room for an altogether different possibility to arise in my experience. Pretty simple, yet it took me a long time to *see* this.

Despite the feedback I was constantly getting from these sensations in my body, my main pre-occupation was with my mind being in resistance to what arose as a useful an effective strategy. Until that realization, I was unconsciously creating more of what I didn't really want. And it was repetitive and unconscious, day in and day out. I noticed that when I became conscious, and allowed any experience to be just the way it was – whether painful or pleasurable, it never owned me; it never stuck around to torment me. I also noticed its life span was very short. Recognizing resistance to anything had to be present for suffering to arise, I stopped resisting!

When I dropped my agenda on insisting that any particular experience conform to how I wanted it to be, a delightful thing happened. Peace and contentment arose – and it stayed. Despite what my mind told me in the past (in regards to allowing and acceptance) this new orientation led to a much more peaceful existence, one that was real and not manufactured from my mind; it began to happen all on its own. Seeing what was real led to new patterns of energy to spontaneously move in ways more in alignment with life.

My experience confirmed this; it was self-authenticating – and things were never the same after that seeing. Fortunately, you can't un-see what you've seen. And once you really see, that seeing *is* *often* the letting go. So, you don't actively "do" surrender. It happens on its own when you *see* (with your conscious awareness) what's true. Letting go happens when we see that what we cling to must bind us. It's as if we are rewarded for seeing what was never true in the first place. When all else goes, truth remains. Truth always remains because truth, being right where you are, never comes and goes. It never left us, as it never arrived.

In fact, whatever comes and goes isn't real to begin with. Reality doesn't come and go. Thoughts, beliefs, opinions, feelings and experiences come and go in the ever-present reality. And since they all come and go, they can't be what you are. Instead of pumping life into a dead thing (a thought of resistance or assertion that something other should or could be happening) by giving it my attention and belief, I would let it die as soon as it arose.

"Let the dead bury the dead" took on a whole new meaning for me. I finally saw its real meaning. It is palpable, too. I could feel a visceral, but startling difference in my experience. I saw that life begets more life, and awareness surely begets more awareness. Contraction previously felt in the body was replaced by an open spaciousness of allowing that felt inclusive and freeing. The more I was consciously aware, and the more I wanted to see, the more freedom and joy I experienced. The more I consciously saw this, the more it was noticed in the next moment.

The more it was noticed, the more it took on a life of its own, without my intention for it to do so. It was like a snowball rolling down a hill, getting bigger and bigger, until at last, you had a solid foundation to make a big snowman. After being tired of being on the carousel of life, spinning around and never getting the ring, I became willing to see what was true. No matter the cost, it didn't matter. I was tired of the suffering and I wanted out. Regardless of what

I thought or feared I'd be giving up (and there was a lot of stuff that came up) I kept looking.

I somehow finally got to the point where I no longer cared about what I "thought" I'd lose; I wanted truth more. *I was done with bringing back the dead, giving life to the dead.* Subsequently, it was much easier to notice when a dead thing arose in my experience, as if it was saying from the grave, "Hey, buddy, give me life with your attention, will ya? Help me out of this hole." Noticing what was vying for my attention, and noticing how differently my life unfolded became enjoyable. When we're sick and tired of being sick and tired, something else moves in and takes over, but only when we've exhausted ourselves, surrendering to our situation.

When we stop dancing with the dead, we notice the dead don't bother us nearly as much. They begin to see that dance partners are few and far between – and we let them rest in peace. Incidentally, this is one of the ways in which grace works. Grace steps in only when we let it step in. It never forces its way in; it waits for us to open the door and invite it in. It waits for us to let go. As Jesus said, *"It is God and not I that doeth the work."* To surrender is to win, not to lose. On the rare occasion that I do get duped now, it is seen rather quickly and discarded, usually before pain arises.

Instead of going to battle with what we don't want, wisdom sees that any time we oppose life we lose. When we stop insisting that our ideas and opinions are actually true, we make room for new possibilities to arise, possibilities more in harmony with our actual experience. In order to sit in a new recliner, we need to discard the old, worn one. We do this by *seeing* the old one no longer serves us. Clearing out the old, we make room for the new.

Fortunately for us, we don't have to continue living out our lives in ways that don't ultimately work for us. Being a conscious and aware species, with the ability to learn and adapt, we can see the error in our ways and choose different in the next moment. The real and original meaning of the word *sin* is to "miss the mark," and not meant to seek control by evoking guilt or shame through the more popular interpretation that has held so many down for centuries.

As long as we sincerely want to be free – and are willing to look until we discover truth more than our fear of losing things we imagine we'll lose, we don't have to miss the mark any longer. With this orientation, we will be a finder, not a seeker. The neat part is that with this conscious orientation of a sincere looking with the intent on finding what's true, we can't help but notice when dead and untrue things present themselves to us, clamoring for our attention.

None of it is a problem unless we believe it is. When we don't say and believe that it's a problem, we watch it pass through, like a fast-moving summer thunderstorm in the middle of July. And what's revealed is the shining sun, the shining sun that was always present, but temporarily obscured. As the Buddha said, *"Three things cannot be long hidden: The sun, the moon, and the truth.*

Chapter 3
Return To Sender

"As one lamp serves to dispel a thousand years of darkness, so one flash of wisdom destroys ten thousand years of ignorance."

~ Hui-Neng

Elephants are truly remarkable and beautiful animals – as are all of God's creations. They possess amazing intelligence, and an uncanny ability to remember. In fact, their memory is so good that it can be very difficult for them to decipher the difference between what's actually taking place, and what isn't. About a year ago, I saw a video clip online of the CEO of Go-Daddy killing a defenseless elephant in Africa, and being very proud of his accomplishment. As I watched in horror, the gunshots dropped the elephant. It made me really sad and angry, especially the way in which the villagers celebrated the death of the magnificent creature.

While I realize that it is much more acceptable in that culture – and what I deemed unacceptable was acceptable to them, I told myself I'd never do business with Go-Daddy again. He got a lot of expected backlash for this and incidentally, sold the company for a huge profit not too long after the uproar. Why does anyone reward these people? Apparently, we don't have to look too far to find those who don't really care about the peripheral stuff; "collateral damage" is acceptable as long as profit is involved, especially large profit. To some, I realize that I am being out of line here with my view, but such is life. Belief in scarcity has driven man to commit many atrocities.

As long as the "overriding outcome outweighs the means," questionable and self-serving behavior often becomes much easier to justify. But let's be honest, there are those who just don't need to justify or rationalize the means, and there's not a whole lot we can do about it. Ignorance is a powerful influencer, and the direct cause for so much bloodshed, is it not? You may be aware that when elephants are being trained by a circus, the trainer controls the massive creature by having a leg shackled with an iron or steel chain. After many months of being trained this way, the elephant not only becomes proficient in the tricks and activities that it's been taught to perform, but comes to believe it's always shackled, even when the shackles are removed.

Once it has been established that the elephant feels it can't get away, the trainer is reasonably confident it will stay put. Instead of going on a rampage or just leaving, the elephant doesn't go anywhere, because it still thinks it's shackled – or at the least believes it's still under the control and influence of the trainer. In other words, *it can't tell the difference between what once was, and what now is.* The elephant still believes it's bound, when in reality it is free to roam as it pleases. The trainer knows just how good the elephant's memory is, and uses it against the elephant, in order to control the elephant.

Enter human beings. Don't we have a very similar problem to that of the elephant? Don't we have an issue with distinguishing the real from the unreal, from truth and falsehood? Don't we allow our memory of the "past" to dictate how we perceive and act in the present? Don't we also possess the key to our freedom, while at the same time feeling imprisoned and shackled? Yes, we most certainly do.

In fact, if we aren't awake to what's real and true, we live our lives from the filter of the past –

which is literally from memory. We keep the past, a dead thing, alive with memory. The truth is, the past does not exist in reality except as memory only. What past is there unless you think about it? Is there one? No, there isn't. Before reading on, *see* this now. If we really look for ourselves, we see that there really isn't a past, unless we think about it.

Since birth, it has been constantly drilled into us that there is a past and a future. Neither has any reality except in our minds. Since the vast majority of us believe the thoughts in our heads, we feel guilt and shame about our past – and fear and anticipate an imagined future. This is the inevitable byproduct of identification with our minds. To be awake and free means to see and realize that *this* moment is all there is, and that anything else is a dream. To be awake and free is to see that time doesn't exist except as a mental construct. In other words, time is mind. It's always *this* moment.

To be awake and free means to live and see *this* moment is all there is. It is prior to thought, memory, belief or opinion – or our interpretation of it. Wisdom blooms when we no longer reference thought or memory to tell us what's true and real. Wisdom blooms when we live in the present moment – where it's NOT possible to suffer. *Wisdom sees that time is mind, and that we can't suffer if we stay in the present, where there is no time.* When we no longer reference the past as something real, we live in the one, true reality

– and nowhere (now here) else. This is the kingdom of heaven Jesus often spoke about.

Have you ever received a package or letter in the mail that you didn't really want by the time it arrived at your doorstep? Perhaps it was an impulse buy, and by the time it was delivered you had a serious case of buyer's remorse? I've done this many times – getting caught, hook, line and sinker by the persuasive presenter telling you it was the best thing since sliced bread! Remember Don Lepre, that dynamic, infomercial salesman back in the mid-eighties and early nineties? He used to do those thirty-minute commercials on television, pitching classified ads as a "simple and lucrative" way to earn money? He'd make earning money seem effortless by posting classified ads in newspapers all across the country for "pennies on the dollar." He'd post ads pointing to some product or service he was selling – and so could you!

The guy was very convincing and you couldn't order fast enough. Well, at least I couldn't. Incidentally, he recently committed suicide due to being in way over his head, apparently having all kinds of legal and financial troubles. Not knowing Don personally, I can't help but sense that intense guilt and shame may have sadly led him to end his life. Perhaps he couldn't envision living with a tarnished reputation, suffering jail time or paying big fines. We'll never know, but it's unfortunate that a guy with all that charm, talent and personality felt the need to take his own life.

So, what do we do when we don't want receipt of that package? We write with big letters on the front, "Return To Sender," don't we? Otherwise, we are stuck with it, right? Fortunately, *we* have the option to return to sender, too. Just as the post office, UPS or Fed-Ex allows us the opportunity to send back (without penalty) what we really didn't want in the first place – but only thought or believed we did – we can do a similar thing with our thoughts, beliefs and habitual patterns of thinking. Just because a thought or belief arises, telling us that something is "true" or desired, we don't have to act on it, do we?

We have the option to return to sender. In this case, the "sender" is our minds, the thing that usually rules the nest, telling us what's best or right. Our minds repeatedly tell us what we "need" in order to be content, safe and secure. And since the majority of our minds believe in scarcity, inadequacy and competition, we hear from it often! The good news is, no matter how convincing these thoughts appear to be – or how persistent they are, it doesn't mean we must take receipt of it.

And yet, if we aren't vigilant and aware, our boxes can get stuffed full. In our state of overload, we have a tendency of our lives becoming one battle after the other. When this happens, we lose sight of the truth that what we battle we only strengthen and sustain. If we are conscious and paying attention to the thoughts and beliefs that arise in us, we give ourselves the ability to see what's really true and real. If not, we will invariably take receipt of so much unreality, paying attention to and dealing with the consequences *after* the fact!

Very often, we don't even see what's *in* our mailboxes because we just can't keep up. Our mailbox (our minds) can be so filled with notions and ideas that have nothing to do with reality that confusion and pain pile up. If we *see* that the vast majority of what we entertain in our minds wasn't even created by us (but taken on board by assimilating what others think we should do) we are in a much better position to see just how ludicrous and unwise our minds can be. If we discern, we can learn.

Again, the mind and its beliefs are never the problem. It is when we *believe and identify with* the thoughts in our minds that problems must arise. When we notice we aren't even doing it, and that it's happening automatically and spontaneously, we give ourselves a much better chance of not getting caught up in it's perpetual web of lies and deceptions. The real meaning of the laughing Buddha is that he finally saw the nature of the mind and its ongoing inability to discern reality versus illusion.

More specifically, he saw through the craziness and insistence of the mind's belief that something other than what is happening, can happen. He saw that the nature of the mind *is* to resist what is – to resist that which is *already* happening was a consistent formula for suffering. Most important, he saw he wasn't the mind, and that he had a mind. As a result, he woke up *from identification with* the mind.

If you received a package in the mail you didn't want – and if you wanted a credit put back on your charge card, would you damage the package and write curse words all over the front in hopes of getting your money back? Would you resist and offend the sender, thinking it's an effective strategy to get reimbursed? Of course you wouldn't. Why would you want to decrease your chances of getting your money back, when all you had to do was write, "Return to sender" and say, "Thanks anyway, maybe another time?" Don't we innately know that kindness and nonresistance can only increase our odds of manifesting our desired outcome?

Likewise, if we don't want the thoughts and beliefs that arise in our experience to stick around and further torture us, we'd be wise to do the same and just thank it for sharing – without resisting it. Granted, we need to be aware of the inevitable and harming nature of the belief in untrue thoughts that arise *before* we can respectfully send them back, don't we? *We can only really "send them back" by first seeing they aren't serving or true, without resisting or avoiding them.* It is in the momentary gap right before we take receipt of anything that we can see what's real versus what's false.

Don't we often intuitively know and sense what's BS and what isn't, especially if we are conscious and willing to look and see for ourselves? I say yes, wholeheartedly. I think you'll agree that you already possess this intuition that has the ability to decipher when bullshit arises. We all possess, in varying degrees of sensitivity, an inner "bullshit-ometer" that goes off, warning us when we're being duped. If we don't always see what's BS at first, and if we don't always see what must ultimately bind us at first, that's absolutely okay and even appropriate – yes, appropriate.

We will see it the next time, or maybe the time after that, who knows? There is no timeline unless we impose one. Is our timeline even real, or is it just a self-imposed thing that runs us? The truth is, the less we make demands of how it should be – the sooner it (seeing what's true) will happen. In an uncluttered room, we are better able to quickly find what we're looking for. When we let go trying to search our mind for the answer, it pops us later when our attention is on something else.

I can tell you this truth without any doubt whatsoever: If you don't *see* whatever it is in any moment that needs to be seen (in order to be free of what binds you) you weren't supposed to see it then anyway. Why? Simply because you didn't! Truth is so simple that the mind has a very difficult time seeing it. As you'll read throughout these pages, minds deal in complexity, and rarely, in simplicity. Did your mind just have something to say about that statement? Did you believe it? Besides, we can only understand what we are first aware of, so there's no need or benefit in beating ourselves up for not seeing it *this* time.

If we are unaware in any moment, how *can* we *see* in that moment? If we are unaware in any given moment, were we really *meant* to see in that moment? No, we were not, so we can relax.

In the spirit of *returning*, let's return to the original topic of this chapter regarding memory, and how our minds see this moment through the filter of the past, and not how it really is. If we really see that past is memory only – and that there is no past unless we think about it – we are way ahead of the game, and in the minority for sure. Seeing these two things clearly, and without any doubt at all serves us in ways we literally can't even imagine. When I finally saw that the past is a mental construct only, with no substance at all – and that unless and until I perceived this moment without any judgment or resistance, I was seeing this moment *from* the past.

Consequently, I was distorting the moment by seeing it *from* the past, from my likes and dislikes – based on my past, and whether or not it conformed to my present agenda. Seeing the unreality of the past (despite the appearance of a past) freed me in ways that's hard to describe. No longer did I have any regrets about "my past," because in seeing there's only the present moment, belief in an actual past dissolved. With that dissolution, so did the negative feelings or thoughts I entertained about that "past."

And here is where the mind has a tendency to step in to argue: What do you mean there's no past? What do you mean that the past is memory only? If that's the case, what is it that gives me the overwhelming impression of time, especially of time past, and of all the things that were? These are all great and reasonable questions. While we can see that it is not possible to live *in* the past or live *from* the past, what is it that convinces us of things of the past? It is memory, and it is memory alone.

While we see that, in our direct experience, there is only an endless present, without beginning, middle or end, there is something that speaks quite clearly and vehemently of things that were – of things which happened moments ago, days ago, months ago and years ago. Again, it is memory. And while we cannot see the past, feel the past or touch the past, we can surely (and quite vividly) remember the past. But we only ever do this in the present moment. Recollecting the past is only ever done right now, is it not?

Memory alone assures me of a past, and if it were not for memory, I'd have no sense of time, either. After all, others have this type of recall of the past and have a clear memory of it as well! Here is where we make the leap and conclude that memory provides us knowledge of an actual past, even if we can't directly *experience* any actual past! And this is where the train leaves the track. We conclude that since we can remember a past, there must *be* a past. We conclude that since having a past feels so real, that it must be real, much like a dream we just woke up from that seemed so real.

We conclude that since we have a strong sense of the past, that there must be an actual past, too. I'm not suggesting memory isn't a good thing. If we didn't possess memory, we wouldn't know that the last time we crossed the road without looking both ways, we almost got flattened by a speeding mail truck. So what could very well happen the next time? We could be road pizza. If we didn't have memory, we wouldn't know that lighting a match in a room filled with leaking gas would be the end of us.

The mystics throughout the ages all agree that when we think of the past, all we really know is a certain memory of it – but that memory itself is always and *only* a present experience. We can remember an incident in our past, but what are we actually aware of? We aren't actually watching that event unfold presently (like *remembering* watching our thirteen year old nephew run eighty yards for a touchdown – go CJ! – but rather, we are watching a present trace or memory of what already happened.

We can only know the past in the present – and as part of the present only. When we *see* this, when we really see this, we see that we can never know an actual past at all. We can only know memories of the past, and those memories exist only as a present experience. *Therefore, when we insist that the "past" actually occurred, it was in truth, a present occurrence and not a past one.* At no point do we ever experience an actual past, because there simply isn't one – except in our memory. Since most of us identify WITH our minds and its functions, we believe in past as reality.

Again, what past is there unless you think about it? Similarly, we can never know or experience the future; we can only ever know anticipations or expectations – which too, are only ever a part of the present experience. Anticipation, imagination and expectation, like memory, are all present facts. They happen presently, and nowhere (now here) else. To see that the past is memory only, and the future as anticipation (both present facts) is to see all time existing now. To *see* the past and the future as nothing but concepts held in the mind, is to *see* the only reality there is – this present moment.

When we *see* this, and I mean *really* see this, we are free because it is not possible to suffer in the present moment. Suffering happens when we believe in a past or future – and when we see this moment from the filter of the past, and not as it is. Suffering only happens in time, and never when we are fully present without stories or agendas. Waking up means to wake up from the concept of time. Sometimes, on the rare occasion that I attempt to share this with those I care for, I invariably get a look like I am from another planet!

Now, I love these people very much, but for whatever reason, apparently they aren't ready or desiring to see this yet. And that's absolutely okay. The truth is, they don't *need* to see this, now or ever. There's no outside agency or force that needs or compels any of us to see this, despite it being open and available to anyone – at any time. At the same time, I must admit the desire does arise now and then to share this, because the lasting byproducts of this seeing are so liberating and joyous. It's like when we found a great restaurant, or saw a wonderful movie; don't we naturally want to share the good news? Since I'm not attached to the outcome – that they see what I'm pointing to – it's not a problem when I see that glazed look that wants to change the subject!

Others have a right to dismiss this as pure lunacy or "out there stuff" that can't possibly be useful to them. Unfortunately, what we dismiss we usually don't look at. Perhaps another day they will look, but either way, it doesn't ultimately matter. I have nothing invested in anyone seeing anything, but if it's truth you're after, we have something to talk about – so bring your empty cup. The mind cannot understand this, but what You Really Are *can and already does*. This can only be understood from within, with Being, and not conceptually in the mind.

When this is truly seen, it is understood energetically in the body. The results are astounding. In other words, the proof is in the pudding, and the saying, "The peace that surpasses all understanding" takes on a whole new meaning because it's your lived experience. It's verified and confirmed by the one who sees what's true and actual. Until then, the mind will continue attempting to reference what's real and true by accessing the concepts and beliefs it clings to – because after all, that's pretty much how we've been taught since day one.

In fact, those who create religion count on this knowing (that we'll continue to look with the mind and rely on belief), instead of our actual experience *of* God or Truth. That's not to imply they know any other way. So, we continue to look to our stored data banks of past "knowledge" to see how it measures up with what we are looking at now. It's literally a habit pattern, a way of thinking and being that continues, until we recognize it's not working for us. We get complacent with the "the same thing, different day" mindset. Until we're no longer content or satisfied with the status quo, or when we sense that there *is* more to see – and more that we *must* see, we won't look any differently.

If we want to live more from truth (than untruth that divides) we do well to bring our awareness back to this present moment – and *return to sender* (mind) the silly notions that catch us off guard and lead us down an unconscious road, a road that generally brings varying degrees pain that drives us into a roadside ditch. Don't be that guy or gal who ends up in a roadside ditch! The more present we are to the thoughts we entertain and cling to, the more we render ourselves powerful in the present moment, the only reality there is. Leaving the land of make-believe (where fantasy is our lived experience) and returning home is always an option that's immediately available.

And when you do, you instantly begin living from truth. If we notice that it's always a timeless now, we have at our disposal an endless opportunity to be in harmony with what is, and not what we imagine what is. The overriding and determining factor becomes *which land* do we really want to live in? Have we suffered enough from living in the land of make-believe, or are we resigned to live our lives the way we always do? There is no right or wrong answer here, and there is no should or shouldn't answer implied here.

That's what's so liberating about all of this. There isn't any punitive God watching over us, keeping score – like Santa. We are free to do and be as we wish, and yet paradoxically, the answer to this question will determine the direction our lives go. Which land we live in will determine the quality of experience – and so much more. If uncomfortable and unwanted feelings and sensations tell us we aren't in harmony with life, then not feeling quite right is a useful and valid indicator. It speaks to us each moment. The question is, do we listen? Do we even *care* to listen?

The activity of returning to this moment (by bringing your awareness back to this moment) to see what's actually happening is essential. This activity of coming back to now, of bringing our awareness back to this moment, is the same thing as *returning to sender*, that which we know doesn't work for us. If the only problem we ever have is to want something other to be happening, wisdom sees that to resist what's happening is counterproductive and painful. It really is that simple.

When we see this moment through the filter of the past and/or how we'd prefer it to be, we are in essence saying, "I really don't want this, so send me suffering." When we take the past to be real, in this moment, we can't ever meet this moment as it is, but only as we'd like it to be. We can't ever escape the byproducts of our interpretations. We can't escape the resulting experience that comes from the way in which we see and interpret. It is just the way it works

– have you noticed? We cannot touch, see or feel anything resembling a past or future.

In other words, in your direct and immediate experience, there is no time – no past or future. There is only an endlessly changing present, shorter than a nanosecond, yet never coming to an end, flashing in and out of existence faster than your eyes can see and perceive. How wonderful to realize that each moment really is fresh and new – and to be lived and experienced knowing it won't ever happen precisely this way again? If you can actually live in the past or future, you'd be the first human to do so. If you happen to figure it out, send me a postcard with precise directions on how to get there, okay?

Chapter 4
No Story, No Suffering

"Man cannot discover new oceans until he has the courage to lose site of the shore."

~ **Unknown**

Have you noticed that animals don't suffer emotionally or psychologically? They might get emotional for a moment, but they don't suffer. I live with a ragdoll cat and a chocolate lab, and I must tell you that it is so refreshing to live with beings that are so even-tempered, greeting each new moment with a wonder and curiosity. Watch your pet and notice how they meet each moment as if it was brand new. Each sight, sound and smell is brand new and not referenced from the past. Who needs a guru or spiritual teacher when you have a pet?

It really is beautiful to watch – and as you may already know, it's contagious. It has been said that our pets are better teachers than our human teachers, and it is very obvious why. They don't tell themselves stories about how things *should* be, and how things *should* unfold. They have no concept of that. Aside from desiring a treat now and then, or going for a walk, they don't go into a fit. When they don't get what they want – or when their preferences are being met, they don't make a big deal out of it.

When a dog feels pain, it yelps. It doesn't go on and on resisting the pain, or tell a story about the pain. Thus, it doesn't suffer. Granted, our pets don't think in the ways we humans do. They certainly don't tell stories, but that's the point. *Because* they don't tell stories or make demands, they don't suffer as we do. We can pinpoint our suffering down to the fact that it is our stories, notions and beliefs about how things ought to be that creates our suffering. Forgive me for stating the obvious again, but isn't it useful to know that we can only understand what we're first aware of?

In other words, if we're in a habitual trance-like state, new possibilities aren't likely to arise. *When we don't see that resistance TO pain causes suffering, we'll continue to resist inevitable pain.* We are creatures of habit and have a tendency to remain with the known, even if the known continues to prove hurtful. Many times, we prefer to stick with the known than venture into the unknown, even if we intuitively know our freedom lies in what we don't yet know.

I once believed a story that I couldn't possibly write a book like this (let alone three), because I believed I didn't have the necessary focus and discipline. I once believed a story that told me I wasn't enough, and that if you *really* knew me, you might not like what you saw, either. As a result, I walked around feeling inadequate and insecure. That story was a long time ago, but you get the point. The only thing we can ultimately do is live out our stories. And, well, sometimes those stories bring suffering because those stories *about* life rarely ever are in sync *with* life. Life is always in flux and always changing, so it's very difficult to nail it down with a static description of it. Besides, concepts and words about a thing only point to a thing, and never can *be* that thing.

If you can just see this – I mean *really* see this, then you are way ahead of the curve. Conversely, we can have empowering stories, too, and we live them out as well. So, if we are faced with no other alternative (when would this be so?) than to live out our stories, it's certainly a better option to make up a good story, as opposed to a not so good one. However, it is still merely a story we are living, which means we aren't directly engaging life as it is. However, there is another option that we can live out, one I didn't see until my late thirties. Apparently, I was wasn't ready to see, or not meant to see it until then – which is essentially the same thing!

This other option is by far the best. And its byproducts are organic and lasting. It's called *no story*, and it doesn't bring suffering because it has no demands or formulas. No one can refute it and there's nothing to maintain. Conversely, any story never intends to meet each moment as it is. It's only interested in desperately keeping alive your story. However, when you live without any story, you live impartially and without mental bias. There's nothing to argue with, including reality. Whether we are aware of it or not, most of us create and maintain stories about our lives so that we can feel safe, secure and in control.

Somewhere along the way, we picked up the idea that to come naked and free, without an agenda, is irresponsible and foolish. Just pick a particular aspect of your life and you will find several underlying stories that serve as buffers to reality, intermediaries between you and the moment. If we can see that we are engaged in our stories about life, and NOT life itself, we give ourselves the real opportunity to transcend our stories. You won't necessarily know how and why these stories were formed, but if you ask it (the story) what it tells you about life, it will.

Each story we have has a voice – and that voice is usually most willing to tell you how it perceives. Believing this voice, we forget that perception is NOT reality. Hence, we live out our perceptions. Our minds love to create stories that have no basis in reality, yet we believe we need them in order to navigate our way through life. They become our compass. You could call it a basic lack of trust. While habitual, it is a still a lack of trust in our own being – and a lack of trust in life, too. Both are essentially the same thing.

The reality is, life is so full of twists and unexpected turns, surprises and mysteries, that when we insist on our stories to explain things – or help us proceed, we often end up feeling confused and emotionally unstable. Our life then, becomes a game of managing our emotional states, up one day and down the next.

We rarely ever look to see whether our stories are true or not, and whether we really would be confused and unstable without them! When we approach aspects of our lives with a story about how it should be, or how it should work out, we literally *ask for* pain and confusion, because our stories seldom match up with how life actually unfolds! We actually think we can box up and compartmentalize aspects of our lives with explanations about them, thinking we can proceed *from* those explanations. Sometimes we put a nice bow on top for good measure, believing it will enhance or our experience, or act as a buffer to our experience.

We manufacture a conceptual reality and superimpose it onto our lives. However, if you were able to completely drop any and all stories about any aspect of your life, it would be literally impossible for you to suffer. Yes, you could be in pain, but that's different from suffering. You wouldn't have a sense of how things should be, or how things *should* work out. Whatever arises would be just fine with you. Whatever outcome would be just fine with you. This is what it means to be awake and free. You are a lover of what is, and don't resist what's already happening. Most minds would insist that this is an attitude of resignation and foolishness.

In truth, it is the true perception that delivers liberation. The Buddha called this, "Right Seeing." Liberation is our experience when we don't insist on our stories about life being adhered to. It's our experience when we don't insist on our personal agendas being fulfilled. In fact, life could care less about the stories we make up, and life could care less if our stories jive with reality. While we suffer from our unmet expectations about life, life continues on, unaffected and free. Remember when Mom or Dad would tell us, "Honey, life just isn't fair?" How right they were, and yet, don't we often insist on life being fair? It's just another belief we create about life (life should be fair) – and when it doesn't match up with our experience, we suffer.

Many times, instead of dropping our concepts about how things should be, we come up with a more clever strategy: When life clashes with our story, just invent a new story! That way, no more suffering and we get what we really wanted all along. As clever as this strategy seems, it's really just a cheap backdoor mind trick. It won't work long term. It may for a while, but inevitably it must fail. That's because when we fail to see that living from a story is ultimately a lie, we don't engage life as it actually is. Disappointment can only ensue.

We actually think life cares about our desires, needs and preferences! It usually takes a whole lot of suffering before we see that this isn't the case, and that something must be truly amiss in our perspective. We start to get a glimpse that just maybe the source of our problem is our interpretations about life, and not life itself. For so long, we don't see that we are reacting to (and living out) the projections we send out through time and space, and not what's actually happening.

We don't fully comprehend the ramifications of our mind's insistence that its conceptual creations actually represent reality and explain how things really are. We somehow believe that we need a secondary interpretation to show us how to be in life. Instead of responding to directly perceived reality, we can recognize we've placed an overlay, a conceptual barrier on the moment, as a way to soften how we experience reality.

We tell ourselves, "Life is just too painful and difficult as it is, so I must come up with a strategy to manage it." When we react to our secondary interpretations, and not directly respond to what is, we usually pay a price. And that's okay, until it isn't okay anymore. Paying a price can definitely serve as a wake-up call for us - to see we are looking in a direction that hurts. Wherever we look is what we'll experience. Simply put, choose the direction and you choose the consequence. However, whenever we suffer, we can use it as a trigger to notice the direction we ARE looking, and choose different.

Each moment is a brand new opportunity to look in the direction that heals - and then to actually look in that direction. In essence, when we don't feel quite right, we are forgetting that our own innate wisdom knows the way - if we would just trust it. Trusting in our own being is not something most of us have been taught to do. Trusting that our own inner wisdom already knows isn't something that most of us have been exposed to. Since we live among other humans that have been conditioned to look to their minds (instead of their hearts) to tell them what's true and real, we naturally do the same thing. We are creatures of both imitation and habit – even if it's not working for us.

Don't we have an inclination to imitate the strategies and approaches of those around us that we admire and respect? How many among us were raised in a culture where we *knew* conceptual understanding is only partial, and therefore, limited and not to be relied on? We've been told that "knowledge is power" – and that the more we accumulate it, the better off we are. When are we ever really taught that knowledge is often, in fact, a barrier that stands in the way of successful living? Instead, we take on board a belief that says, "We need to first understand a thing conceptually in order to proceed accordingly."

Implicit in this view is that our innate wisdom isn't enough and knowledge is king. Granted, to the mind that deals in conceptual reason and belief, this makes sense. While conceptual understanding can be very useful in a certain contexts and life situations, it is usually quite limited when it comes to the bigger issues in life. *Inner wisdom already knows, while our minds think it needs to attain more concepts in order to really know.* What would it be like to just show up in this moment, in an open state of discovery, without any story or agenda?

What might it be like to be in this moment, without any beliefs, conclusions or ideas – with a complete willingness not to know anything at all? Don't answer this question with a conceptual answer. Find out for yourself in your actual experience. Initially, this scenario may seem very scary, and yet, there are times when we do just this – meet the moment as it is. When we do, we notice that "we" aren't in the picture; "we" aren't part of the equation. We find that we are much more present when our agenda is absent.

In the absence of any agenda, we are truly present. In fact, whether we realize it or not, there are many occasions where we simply forget ourselves, where we are most present when we are absent. If we are honest with ourselves, we see that in order to fully show up in our lives, a dropping of any and all agendas, opinions and preferences is needed. Then and only then, are we really Here, meeting this moment on *its* terms, not ours. Besides, where has believing in dogma, scripture and other sources of "wisdom" really gotten us? Where has it gotten us, other than temporary and fleeting relief and a false sense of security – the kind that comes and goes? Doesn't that seem manufactured and unreal to you, and therefore, tell you something about its authenticity?

Possessing the perception that *"whatever wants to arise is just fine by me"* is the way of freedom, the way of enlightenment. This may seem a scary proposition to the mind. To come unarmed and without an agenda, may even seem weak and resigning. However, check it out in your own experience, instead of what your mind tells you about it. This pointer isn't for your mind. This is for YOU. Minds will go to great lengths to convince you something is true when it's not. And it's not a problem. You won't be successful if you consciously create a story that says, "I am just fine with whatever arises." This perception will spontaneously happen once you've seen through all you're your illusory stories, beliefs, assumptions, etc.

As long as we continue to identify with the mind, we won't ever see this. We just need to take that extra step, and look and see for ourselves what's actual. Having a good dose of humility will prevent us from thinking we are stupid. If we don't humble ourselves, we're less likely to look. Because we're identified with the mind, we fear what we'll tell ourselves about our intellectual capacity. We just create another story to live from. Unless we're willing to come naked and free, never will we see that it's all just a defense against nothing.

Not all stories are disabling. As we discussed, if we must create a story, we can create an empowering one. There's nothing wrong with this, at least not temporarily. Using what we need to use for a time isn't shameful, nor does it make us any less worthy. Life is game of seeing and not seeing. The more you see what's real, the less pain and division you experience. It really IS that simple. Like belief, a story can serve as a bridge, until we no longer need that bridge to get across to the other side. Sometimes that bridge collapses, and we are left clinging to its railings. It's a good indicator that we must go beyond belief, because we know that ultimate and lasting freedom IS beyond any story we can come up with.

When we insist that our stories, agendas and desires need to be manifested, our lives become problematic. Desire in and of itself isn't the problem. Many people are under the impression that the Buddha said that "desire is the root of all suffering." He never said this. Buddha said that, "attachment *to* desire is the root of all suffering." Quite a big difference! Being human, desires will arise and desires will fall. Nothing would get done; advancements in medicine and technology wouldn't occur in the absence of desire. Procreation wouldn't happen in the absence of desire – and perhaps you wouldn't be reading this now!

However, when we insist that our personal desires need to be met in order for us to be happy, we must suffer to some degree. Do we believe in order to be happy or content, our desires must be met? Do we really believe that fulfilling our desires is the key to lasting and real happiness? Does your intuition tell you that a life lived demanding all desires met can only be an empty life? Whenever we insist or demand anything, we can be sure that suffering will follow, like night follows day.

Life just doesn't work this way; life doesn't cater to what we desire. It's *we* who need to desire what life brings, for if we resist how the moment unfolds, *we* suffer. Desiring what Is, is the way of the liberated and free. Wisdom recognizes that having only preferences is the way to live in harmony with our experience. All of this can be experimented with and confirmed in your direct experience. Don't believe a thing you ever read here, and find out what happens when you insist on getting your desires met. See that wanting what you have is freedom. See that having only preferences is freedom. See that the truest freedom is not wanting.

In order to be vigilant against creating stories in our lives that invariably lead to division and pain, there are a few things we can do without applying effort or actual "doing." Telling the truth is one powerful way that takes no effort. Somehow, as a species, we've perfected pretending as a way of being – as if telling ourselves the truth is a scary thing to avoid. The funny thing is that truth needs no defense, while stories and beliefs do! Once we've aligned ourselves with truth, the armor naturally falls away.

No longer are we in protection mode, because we have truth on our side. We've become great pretenders, and it goes mostly unnoticed because it is such a common practice. Everyone does it, so it must be okay, right? Somehow, we've come to believe that telling the truth is a difficult thing to do, and that it usually brings consequences we'd rather not face. We may conclude that lying to ourselves (and others) is easier and less painful. We hurt most when we deceive ourselves. We forget that it's really difficult to be honest with others when we deceive ourselves.

Often times, what is true in a situation is that we really don't know - and in fact, really can't know. But we've been conditioned early on to believe not knowing is a bad thing, a weak thing, an unenlightened thing. The reality is nothing could be further from the truth! Uncertainty is an integral part of the natural order of life, and to deny this reality is to invite chaos and confusion. If we have the humility and earnest willingness to notice that it's our mind's function to resist the unknown (this present moment) - and that it's our mind that has a constant *need to know* - we are better able to tell the truth and admit when we don't know.

More critically, we are better able to SEE that we *can't* know anything in this brand new moment, because this fresh moment has nothing to do with what came before. Granted, it feels that way and our perceptions tell us otherwise. However, the reality is that this moment stands independent of the moment that just died. Until then, we will identify with our thinking minds (that needs to know) and continue to lie to ourselves, pretending we know when we don't.

We will play out our lives much in the same way as we did before. It's all one big charade.

When we are willing to see what's true, no matter what, we recognize that we can't possibly know. We can only imagine we know. When we disengage with the ego that pretends to know – and must know, when we see the ego's need to project a certain image, ego's grip is loosened. What we think is, and what actually is, are not the same. We over-look this fact all the time! If we drop all stories, we see that, in our experience, not knowing is quite peaceful and expansive. The experience of not knowing isn't what we've been told it is – or what we've imagined it is. You might find that it's spacious and peaceful – and where true and unlimited potential originates.

The unknown (no story) is so much more peaceful than ever imagined – and not something to run and hide from. *Whenever we're willing not to know, we refrain from identifying with the mind's unexamined conclusions and allow ourselves to be in an open state of discovery. If truth demands anything at all, it demands an open state of discovery and an innocent looking filled with curiosity and wonder.* Is this moment weak and without power? What does it need? Does it need our help or guidance? When we insist that we know anything in this moment (except for the fact of our own being, that we exist) we are in fact, bringing the past to *this* moment. We bring to life a dead thing and attempt to resurrect it.

When we think we know anything in this moment, we aren't seeing the reality of this moment. This moment has no story, and it has no suffering. It is devoid of anything stale or old. It is our minds that bring stories – and consequent suffering, to this moment. This moment literally need nothing other than your showing up to it, without an overlaying secondary interpretation of it. It doesn't even "need" us to show up to it. That's on us! Stay out of your mind, be fully present, and see this for yourself. Don't rely on another. There is nothing more liberating, I tell you. No story, no suffering.

Another thing we can do, instead of believing in a need to create a story around something (or notice that a limiting one is already in operation), is to just be curious about what is true in the moment. It is this orientation of curiosity and not knowing that is such a powerful and peaceful combination that baffles the mind – if you allow it. Be like your pet and show up innocently to this fresh and new moment. Act as if it will never repeat itself in that way – because it won't. It is the mind's habitual belief that it "knows" what's happening. This very belief causes so much boredom for the mind because it thinks it's the same old thing!

We're only bored when we come from the mind. The mind believes peace and security comes from knowing (or strongly believing in) something. This is no surprise (as the mind needs to know) and will go to *any* lengths to avoid not knowing! YOU are not the mind. You precede the mind, and therefore, you have a mind. Call it Awareness or Spirit that animates your body and mind if you prefer. Without referencing thought, what are you really?

You are the silent, aware presence that everything arises from and falls back into. Believing you *are* the mind is the problem – the problem that causes *all* problems.

This can't be seen conceptually, with your mind, but YOU can see this now. The mind's need to know at all costs often overshadows the more natural impulse we have of just resting in curiosity, examining what's really true or not. If we have a natural inclination to always have to explain things when we really don't know, we can use that tendency (when it comes up) as a trigger to just relax and be okay with not knowing. The alternative is just to be reactive and repetitive – and let the mind lead the way. As the mind goes, you go.

Life will unfold as it unfolds anyway, regard-less of the way in which we would like it to unfold. If we really desire to live in harmony with life, and if we really desire more peace and less angst, we do well to pause in that gap, that gap right before we hop on that train of belief in our story. It is in this small gap where we can either go unconscious and suffer the consequences, or be aware of that gap (of no story) – and enjoy the peace that comes with resting in that.

Aware that we have options in any moment, and aware that we aren't automatons without any volition at all gives us the wherewithal to look in a different direction. With awareness, comes volition and choice. Trusting in our own innate sense of wisdom, our own being, takes us a long way. When we see that life has no story, and that life knows how to live better than our egoic minds do, we become more conscious. When we see that there's no separation between life and what we really are, we let go and naturally trust. When we believe we are separate from life, we naturally don't trust.

The great news is that the more we show up and remain in the here and now, we realize that no story was ever needed. We see that the moment lacks nothing at all – and it never does. *The more we notice that our being always and already remains in the now, the easier it is to just rest.* It was just our minds that told us that we're separate from the moment. And we believed it. In truth, there's just the next thing that's happening. There's always just the next thing that's happening. I don't mean to say "next" in terms of future next, but right now. As soon as right now is experienced, the next thing is experienced, right now. Sometimes the next thing that's happening is some-thing that your mind says is good that it wants, and sometimes the next thing is something that the mind says is not good, and you don't want.

But either way, none of the thoughts about what's happening have any validity to them, positive or negative. A nonsensical notion – but it's nonetheless, true. Find out. Since seeing this doesn't require us to think rationally, or in a linear fashion, reason and logic don't have to factor in. In fact, in this case, they don't at all. What you think is happening doesn't equate to what's happening. What's happening is just what's happening, prior to the concepts our minds create.

We get endless opportunities to see and experience what is as it is, before or independent of, any story about it. No matter what it is, it's not a problem, until the mind tells itself a story about what's happening. Only when the mind talks to itself about what is happening, what has happened, or what may happen, does stress, anxiety or suffering happen. The mind has conversations with itself about what is happening all the time. The mind converses with itself about what it would like to have happen, or must have happen, all the time. And yet, when we turn on the evening news and discover that a serial killer heard voices in his head, telling him to kill, we say he's evil and insane!

We are all insane (in varying degrees) and fortunately, the vast majority of us don't hear voices that tell us to murder. The sooner we admit this, the sooner we can get on with the business of happy living. Thought itself isn't the problem. Stories themselves aren't the problem. Problems arise when we believe in our thoughts and stories to be accurate representations for reality. They never are. When the light of conscious awareness penetrates any story of ego-based suffering, the story no longer continues to be the final authority. No story, no suffering.

Chapter 5
When Wisdom Blooms

"Wisdom tends to grow in proportion to one's awareness of one's own ignorance."

~ Anthony de Mello

Ever since I was young, I've had a desire to know who I am, why I am here, and what is true. At times, it was bordering on obsessive. The older I got, I noticed I was more naturally drawn to spirituality than religion. Being an avid reader, I consumed everything I could get my hands on. I can honestly say that the desire to know the answers to these questions has been extinguished. Seeing that answers are for the mind that needs to know, and seeing that I am not my mind, those questions dissolved. This is not to imply I've reached some end point (there isn't one) or that I am no longer open to Life and all its beauty and wonder.

In fact, the opposite is the case, as I am very open to life; each moment is fresh and new. Besides, there's no such thing as "having all the answers." Books and listening materials played a big part in my journey. While the "answers" aren't found in books and tapes, I'd be lying to you if I said that they didn't serve a useful role, because they did. I can't tell you how many books I've read since my late teens that had to do with self-help and spirituality.

I read and gained insight from some of the more popular self-help giants; Tony Robbins, Zig Ziglar, Og Mandino, Dan Millman, Wayne Dyer, Deepak Choprah and Earl Nightingale. Being raised Roman Catholic in a moderately religious family, I read much of the New Testament and the teachings of Jesus, to some of the great Christian mystics like Meister Eckhart, C.S Lewis, Henri Nouwen, Mother Theresa, Peace Pilgrim, Brother Lawrence, Thomas Merton and Anthony de Mello. Perhaps my favorite all-time quote is from Francis of Assisi. Not only was he a lover of all life – especially nature and animals, he gave one of the most direct and accurate pointers to Truth, *"What you're looking for is what's looking."*

For about 5-6 years, I immersed myself in "A Course in Miracles", "Conversations with God", and Ernest Holmes' "Science of Mind". I enjoyed and resonated deeply with the writings of Vietnamese Buddhist Monk, Thich Nanh Hanh, to the Sufi poets Hafiz, Kabir and Rumi. In 1998, Eckhart Tolle's book, *The Power of Now* hollered at me from the shelves in Borders Bookstore – and it led to the end of seeking. From there, I was led to the 20th century Indian Sages, Nisargadatta Maharaj, Ramana Maharshi and Papaji.

I share all this only to illustrate that my journey was as varied as the teachers and teachings I was exposed to. I include them all in my heart as equally appropriate and valuable, and am deeply grateful for their unique input and guidance. Despite some teachers having more of an impact than others, none are more worthy than the next. Whatever teacher and teaching I was drawn to at the time was exactly where I was supposed to be at the time. Looking back, it is certainly mysterious how it all unfolded, yet plain to see that my own inner wisdom was guiding me in directions I couldn't fully comprehend.

I only knew one thing and it was this: I wasn't going to stop seeking until I knew I found home. Something within told me I would know when I knew, like when you know you're in the right place at the right time, or when you just know you've met the right person you'll spend the rest of your life with. I wasn't going to stop until belief was no longer relied on to tell me what was true. I wasn't going to stop until something within told me I had found what I was looking for. I knew it wouldn't be conceptual knowing – and that it had to be an experiential knowing.

Nothing less than a permanent shift in my being and the way I perceived would do. In the early nineties (in my mid-twenties) I walked on 1200-degree hot coals with Anthony Robbins, without burning my feet. While I felt no pain or burns from that fifteen-second walk, high-fiving a fellow participant *after* the walk was very painful! That experience opened my eyes to the power of my mind and the power of focus. From about the ages of 18 to 26, the majority of the materials I read and listened to were self-help in nature.

I even spent a good chunk of attention and energy with a humanistic movement called, "Lifespring" – a movement similar to EST and the The Forum. Over the next decade, when I had the strong sense that I was spirit having a human experience, the majority of materials I consumed were spiritual in nature. I am 47 now, and rarely do I ever pick up a book. If I do, it is for the sake of enjoying how others point to the one Truth, and to say, "Ah yes, that's it."

Again, it's not that I have all the answers. How deluded is that? Besides, there's no such thing as "having all the answers." It's just that the energy of seeking dropped away, along with the desire to read what others have to say about spirit. But here's my point: For years, I read and read about what others had to say *about* self-improvement, spirituality and enlightenment – and much of it resonated deeply within. But it wasn't until I really looked within, that I discovered what I was looking for. It wasn't until I looked in the direction that some of these people were pointing to, that real and lasting transformation occurred.

We can read and read concepts until the cows come home, but unless we look in the directions we are being pointed to, *from those who have already realized the truth of their true nature,* not much will change for us. This is what I did for so long; I didn't look. Once a book or audio was finished, for a short period of time afterwards, peace and flow was my experience. But not long after, my life returned to the status quo – and I'd feel disillusioned and confused. It wasn't until my later thirties that I realized why.

Seeing that there is only now, and that past and future are just imaginary concepts created in the mind, brought about a peace and contentment that surpasses all understanding. If things are falling apart around me, it's still okay. It's not a mindset, either. If superiority or judgment arises – or if arrogance arises (especially spiritual arrogance, like I *know* and you *don't*) I know that in that instant, I am identified with ego.

Being temporarily identified with ego that compares and divides – and not spirit that includes and unites, just by noticing it, it lets go. Meeting it disperses it. Laughing at it, as if to say, "nice try, ego" is all that's really needed. The beautiful thing is that often the seeing IS the letting go. Humility has a way of putting you right back to where you rightfully belong – right here, right now, eternally in Spirit, always in grace; no better or worse than another. Without grace, nothing is. Without grace, I am not. Inner wisdom is an ineffable, subtle thing. We all have it, and most of us have very little idea how to access it because we're so busy focused on the drama of life, and the things that come and go.

I am by no means a basher of the self-improvement movement. It certainly has a useful and beneficial role in the proper context, at least temporarily. Undoubtedly it has helped many, myself included, but I do see the inherent flaws in it. There's nothing wrong with leaning on something if we need to, just as long as we know we can't rely on it forever. If we break our ankle, we are wise to use crutches until we can walk on our own. However, the basic supposition in the majority of self-help programs, books and other materials, is that we need help and that the separate self needs repairing.

Self-help can be likened to a ladder leaning against a wall that goes up to a rooftop. And on that rooftop is where you want to be, or where your end goal is. The prize sits at the top, and you must ascend the ladder to get to it. Put another way, you don't presently have whatever it is that's on the rooftop. You must begin a process to learn the steps to acquire the information needed. You climb each rung, one at a time, until finally you reach the top – your end goal.

The assumption is that you don't already know what you need to know in order to attain the goal. Therefore, you need to purchase the information authored by someone who has already traversed the path. Tony Robbins was the master at this. He reportedly got everything he wanted in a short amount of time. After living in a 400 square-foot apartment, washing his dishes in the tub, he had an epiphany one day. If he just modeled the success of others, he'd have what they have. Simple enough, right? Why reinvent the wheel?

Just study Richard Bandler and John Grinder, the founders of Neuro-Linguistic Programming – or NLP, and you're off in the right direction. Ask the right questions in order to get the right answers, master public speaking in a dynamic way and never give up. As a result, you'll have what less than one percent has! Finally, write out your goals on the back of a map one day while traveling on a high speed train in Europe – and presto, a short, eighteen months later, the world is your oyster. Not too long after, you're flying around in your own private jet, doing speaking engagements worldwide for $100K a pop.

Now granted, much of this is tongue and cheek, and I'm oversimplifying here. I don't mean to suggest Tony is completely off his rocker or in-authentic, because I don't sense that he is. How-ever, teaching others how to live a life continually managing their states takes a whole lot of effort. The strategies employed are manufactured and must have a certain life span. And I don't mean to imply that many haven't already benefited from this approach – because they have. But when it comes to letting our innate wisdom bloom, or realizing what we really are, this approach will always fall short and fail to deliver – simply because it must.

When we seek lasting happiness with material riches, avoiding pain and gaining pleasure, when we base our contentment on things outside of ourselves, we set ourselves up for misery. Lasting contentment can *only* come from within, and from what's true and permanent. It's an organic approach based on life's demands, not ours. So, when I mentioned that I made the switch from self-help books and tapes to spiritual books and tapes, I said it was because I had a strong sense that I was Spirit – and not what I appeared to be, a separate human individual, amongst other human individuals, living in this world. With that sense came my own sort of epiphany in the form of a visual metaphor one night as I lay in bed.

I likened my life not to a ladder I had to ascend to attain something I thought would bring me lasting fulfillment, but to a rose, mostly un-bloomed, but here for the purpose of blooming. The purpose or reason for my life on earth then, was to blossom into what I somehow knew I already and eternally was, undivided Spirit, already unified, already whole and complete – and inextricably free. I knew that wisdom – not intellectual knowledge, was the power or energy that would reveal the shift I was seeking. I saw that knowledge served its purpose and was appropriate in certain contexts and life situations.

However, it was wisdom and truth that I was after. Intuitively, there was a sense that told me that I already *knew* what was essential to live a happy and peaceful existence. That knowing sense told me I just needed to see what was in the way of that wisdom and truth revealing itself as who I am. Simply put, I needed to provide the proper conditions for it to blossom. I knew that the more conscious and aware I became, the more that wisdom bloomed. I knew it wasn't a process of learning, because learning implied that I didn't already know. I knew that it was more a process of *unlearning* – a process of subtraction and removing what was covering over what was already known. I can tell you many years later that this metaphor has proved true in so many ways.

Although there really isn't any "journey" needed to arrive to the only reality – right now, my own spiritual journey has taken many twists and turns. As I look back, it is really quite remarkable how one teaching and teacher led to the next. I can't say that I'm still a seeker today because it's known that this moment is it – and this moment isn't lacking anything at all. And it's never completed. This moment is endless. In fact, it is never over as *this never-ending present moment* lasts forever, eternally. You may think this is my belief. It isn't.

Eternally doesn't mean forever in time; it means outside the stream of time and space, where there is no beginning, middle or end. Here's a good metaphor to explain this: Imagine listening to a group of people chant the word, "NOW" without ever stopping. Can you hear it? This is the timeless present, and everything (including thought, feeling and experience) arises in and falls back into this timeless now, in that chanted sound we call NOW. There is a real and lasting contentment here that resulted from taking a heart approach, and not a conceptual approach in the mind laden with belief and dogma.

All the books I read were mostly read in a conceptual way, from the discriminating mind that evaluated and compared – and not from below the neck, impartially and innocently, where true wisdom resides. I wasn't really looking in the direction I was being pointed, either. Apparently, I didn't see the importance at the time. I later discovered that when I read from my head and not my heart, I stayed at that level, in my head. Truth is never found or realized in the mind. If there's only one thing you "believe" or take on "faith" in this book – until you see it for yourself – believe this.

While this may sound confusing, I hope you at least get a glimpse of what I am pointing to here, because it *really is* critical to see. If you don't now, please do not be concerned. The realization will occur when it's meant to occur. No striving or pressure needed; this will only prevent you from seeing! This *seeing* isn't abstract in any way, but experiential and sensed in the body. Abstractions reside in and from the mind, but what we seek is beyond the mind, and therefore, can't be realized *with* the mind. Discovering that real transformation happens below the neck and not from the inherently limited, conceptual thinking is the aim here.

The philosophy *about* something isn't the actual, is it? Philosophy, comprised of words and concepts, only points to something far greater; it isn't the actual. What ultimate good is philosophy if we haven't realized what we've read or contemplated? If our "knowledge" stays at the level of our minds – and not our hearts, we won't benefit in the long run. *No longer being satisfied with NOT having an actual lived experience of what I read, ultimately led to experiential knowing.*

I wanted the real thing, and I became willing to look wherever I was being pointed. I mean, what benefit is it to us if our "wisdom" is based on concepts and beliefs – and what outside "authorities" claimed? If I didn't experience it directly for myself, what those authorities claimed meant nothing. If I didn't know it from within, I didn't know it. This dissatisfaction felt in the body, coupled with a burning desire to simply *experience* God or Source (and not just collecting thoughts *about* God or Source) was the catalyst for a different kind of seeing – one where real wisdom was accessed.

One day, I came across a question that hit me like a ton of bricks. It read, "What is your actual experience of God?" It wasn't, "what do you know of God", but "what is your actual and direct experience of God?" Reading that question became the moment when my course was forever altered. The manner in which I became so willing to look where I was invited to look took on a whole new dimension; nothing less than truth would suffice. It was that moment when I saw the inherent limits of religion and belief, concepts, scripture, sutra and dogma.

Since I didn't want more of what I was getting, I wasn't willing to continue to delude myself any longer. I knew a different approach was needed if I was to be a finder and not a seeker. It occurred to me to ask, "what's the point of being a seeker if I didn't have a sincere intent on finding?" I soon discovered that when I looked in the directions that were being pointed to (from *below* the neck, and not with my analytical and comparative mind that evaluated what it *thinks* it knows from past experience) that something energetic within was activated; I felt an actual and organic shift in consciousness that played out in my body and affairs.

And it wasn't conceptual in nature. When it's not conceptual, it has a real chance of being transformative and life - changing. There was no doubt present. If it *was* conceptual in nature, it had to include belief. And if belief was involved, a certain level of doubt had to be present. Time usually tells the real story. Over time, I noticed that doubt still didn't arise. I found that the realizations were experiential and organic, taking on a spontaneous life of its own – only known and understood from the inside out.

When it was suggested that I don't look with the mind, confusion often arose. I remember feeling confusion and thinking, "What do you mean, don't look with the mind...how else *would* I look, how else *can* I look?" So, the pointers can seem very abstract and confusing, tempting us to throw them out as a ludicrous waste of time. My suggestion would be don't throw the baby out with the bathwater. Just keep looking. Since most of us look to our minds to tell us what's true, of course it may seem ludicrous at first – *because* we don't understand it.

So, if there is confusion with this suggestion, just know it's very common. It does appear abstract, especially when approached by the thinking mind, but it isn't. This is a very different kind of looking – the kind that is rarely taught and the kind that doesn't rely on the mind. Besides, most of our accepted ways of discovering haven't really delivered on their promises. We've got nothing to lose, except everything that is untrue about us. And when everything that is untrue falls away, truth remains. This is *always* game of subtraction, not addition.

If your mind has something else to say about this, I invite you to suspend your judgment. Refrain from throwing it out as something not worthy of your attention, because in truth, there's not much more that *is* worthy of your attention – this type of looking, I mean. This kind of looking is way more transformational, and its benefits are lasting and real. One great byproduct is that once you've seen the truth of something, you can't un-see it. Once you've truly seen the truth of something, it can no longer have any power over you. Anything we're conscious of can never harm us; it's the things we're unconscious of that harms us.

What we're conscious of can no longer torture or cause us suffering because we don't give it life with our confusion or resistance. Just keep it simple and know that anything still in the dark recesses of our consciousness has the ability to divide us; anything seen and met out in the open light of awareness can't. Our job is to simply meet what's causing us division – and watch it melt away. Notice when the mind steps in to give its thoughts and judgments. When it does, just let it be. It's not a problem unless you make it one. Someone once said, *"The only problems we have are the ones we believe in."* How true.

This is a game of subtraction, allowing and looking to see what's actual. A good way to tell if you're looking with the mind, as opposed to your heart, where wisdom resides, is that you'll notice your mind agreeing, disagreeing and judging what it's looking at based on the accumulation of past concepts believed to be true. This is what the mind does – and this is one of its many functions. It evaluates what arises presently in relation to what already arose – and then compares both to its manufactured model of reality based in belief and separation.

In other words, when we are invited to look in a direction that is different from what we're accustomed to – and we find ourselves comparing it against our likes and dislikes, we can be sure we are looking with the mind and not the heart. The heart, being a lover of what is, looks on without preference or partiality – without discrimination or distinction, for it knows the way is the way of acceptance and inclusion – and not resistance, avoidance and comparison. You may have read this conceptual pointer before, but have you REALLY investigated and confirmed it experientially for yourself – as if your life depended on it? While your physical life may not depend on, the quality of your overall life certainly does.

If resistance or grasping is happening, it's a telltale sign you're looking with the mind. Wisdom sees that separation is the grand illusion – and notices it is the mind that separates and divides. Reality doesn't divide. What you really are doesn't divide. By dividing and believing in the appearance of separation, we feel this fracture in our direct experience – with an unmistakable felt sense of inner division. This isn't a bad or wrong thing at all. It is just a reminder that we are indeed, looking with the discriminating mind that habitually leans heavily towards what it's most comfortable with – even if it brings pain!

Minds resist the unknown at all costs; have you noticed this? When we aren't in harmony with life, our bodies tell us instantly. It's telling us that we aren't in harmony with what is. All that is needed is to be aware of it, and to see that we are looking in the direction of what's true. With our awareness, we turn and face the proper direction (like West if we wish to enjoy the sun-set) while dropping our insistence of playing out our habitual tendencies. And we simply notice the experience of that.

Most of us unknowingly suppress our natural wisdom that just needs to be approached in the right way in order to blossom. Can a flower blossom without sunlight, water and proper soil? Of course it can't. If you wanted to feed the pigeons while sitting on a park bench, would you aggressively throw breadcrumbs in their direction in hopes of attracting them, or would you nonchalantly toss them lightly in their direction, gently welcoming them? Our approach makes a big difference.

We are constantly exposed to countless ideas and strategies that suggest ways to access the inner wisdom we all naturally possess. We read, listen to and ingest those ideas from all kinds of people, but not much changes for us. It's disillusioning and confusing, and it can lead to resignation and despair. If wisdom is something we already possess – and NOT something we need learn, it follows that *how we orient ourselves* (with the intent of accessing this wisdom) is essential, wouldn't you say? If gaining access, or tuning into our own inner wisdom is something that brings more peace and meaning to our lives, paying attention to *how* we go about it, is also essential, wouldn't you agree?

As the popular saying goes, "if nothing changes, nothing changes." If we go about our business as usual, we will inevitably get more of the same, won't we? If we want to enjoy the sunrise, we must be facing east, or we won't enjoy that sunrise. Likewise, if we want to live from the wisdom we already possess, we must look in the direction that wisdom demands. While it is neutral and unbiased, it demands we look in its direction. Its attitude is like, "Hey, I am eternally here if you need me" – and never, "Hey dummy, look here, I'm getting impatient." It's worth repeating, so at the risk of being repetitive, here goes: If wisdom is below the neck and isn't conceptual, we must look from our hearts, not our heads.

When I finally saw that believing the thoughts in my head was a surefire way to suppress my natural state of wisdom, something happened. When I questioned everything that I thought was true, something else happened. When I was fully present in this moment, without any investment on "my way" being the outcome, something *really* different happened. This *something that happened* continued to happen as long as I kept with this kind of looking. Notice I didn't say, "mindset." The approach is from being that already knows; the approach is one that's intent on seeing what's true, uncovering what's already there – and not from an analytical mind that depends on logic, reason and the past.

When I met the moment, without any investment in things being a particular way, I noticed a feeling of spacious freedom that was very welcoming and inclusive. When I no longer believed the thoughts in my head, and was willing not to know anything at all, that spacious freedom was present again. I began to really enjoy the freedom that came about as a result of making no demands on the moment. It started to take on a life of its own, without my conscious intent. When I saw that life didn't need my help, an ease of being was felt I hadn't felt before.

When I saw that life really was so much more capable of living in an effortless way than I was, I was able to hand over the keys, roll down the window and just *enjoy the ride*. And then, another interesting thing began to occur. I saw that when I no longer referenced my mind to tell me what's true, and trusted in my own being to know how to live life, life flowed in ways I hadn't experienced before. This confirmed that there really wasn't any separation. And it often took the path of least resistance. I liked that because that was my style! I never bought into the popular notion that you had to "work hard" to achieve what you wanted. Wisdom and the path of least resistance, the one without a lot of striving and effort, always seemed to go hand in hand.

As a result, it occurred to me to just say YES to what was already happening. That seemed very sane to me; *rejecting what was already happening seemed like real insanity to me*, the kind that got lunatics locked up for good! So this seemed like true wisdom, and it was confirmed in my experience. When I no longer argued with reality, I felt relaxed and free. Surely this was wisdom! I was home, at last. Allowing what is, to be *as it is,* felt strange initially.

However, it soon became the norm. No longer did I buy into the belief that said I was "giving up or giving in" when I allowed something to occur that I didn't prefer. No longer did I believe that I had to "fight for" what I wanted (if at first my way) didn't manifest itself. This belief dropped away when I saw the truth of things, that resisting and fighting what was *already actually occurring* only prolonged what I didn't want. I was tired of the pain and suffering, and losing in life. I wanted to win in life; I knew that in order to win, I had to work with myself, not against myself.

When I dropped the fight, I began to win in a big way. Let me rephrase that so it's more accurate: seeing that opposing life was a losing situation, the fight dropped away. What a beautiful paradox, and in fact, I began to see that ALL of life was a beautiful paradox. I could just allow what was happening, *as* I intended for something more desirable to happen, if that was the case.

Life began to flow with such ease because I was living in harmony with it, trusting that life really does know best. I saw that sometimes life went through hell in order to come out the other side. I was okay with that, too, because wisdom told me that life knew better than I did – so if life chose going through hell that day, then going through hell that day was indeed the way. My mind, being a finite thing, couldn't comprehend the infinite.

Instead, I deferred to a different kind of looking and experiencing, because I finally decided to actually confirm for myself what the enlightened were attempting to convey. I discovered that I could not pick and choose what I liked and didn't like; I had to stay with the same orientation in all aspects of my life. I didn't have the luxury of saying, "Hey, I'm okay with this being *this* way in this part of my life, but I'm not okay with being this way with *that* way in that part of my life" – AND thinking I'd still be free. I had to include the whole lot – or I'd suffer. It was very consistent.

I noticed that there's only one thing going on. I noticed that I couldn't fool life, either. Being okay with life choosing the route through hell made for a short ride, a ride without many bumps and bruises. Sometimes it's necessary to go through the jungle to get to the land of paradise, but the key was being okay with being in *either* land. As a very good friend of mine once said, "It's easy to know NOT to get caught up in hell, but it isn't so easy to know *not* to get caught up in heaven." How profound. Both are okay with me, as both are temporary experiences anyway.

Without insisting on my preferences being met, or offering resistance to what is, experience would never torture me. Wisdom sees that nothing remains – that everything comes and goes. By allowing the natural and cyclical order of things to do its thing – and function the way it does, I was no longer resisting what was actually happening. And I couldn't suffer, either. That was the really cool part – noticing that I could confirm this for myself and not have to rely on others to tell me what was true. What a relief!

One of things that we are so enveloped in (and run from at the same time) is innately so full of wisdom. It is silence. Silence is often seen as the enemy, or at the least, something to be avoided. When we make friends with silence, we can't help but have wisdom bloom inside us. Wisdom is rooted in silence and silence is rooted in wisdom. Wisdom sees that silence is the ground of all being, and that silence is, in fact, what each moment arises from and falls back into. If you just look for yourself, you'll notice each sound you hear arises from silence and falls back into silence. Each thought you speak comes from silence, and then falls back into silence.

You see this in your experience – and not with your mind. Confirm this now. We can't ever escape silence, yet somehow we've concluded it's not always our friend! How many of us run from silence, the backdrop of each and every moment? How many of us look to be entertained and distracted with television, books, music, food, sex, drugs and alcohol, in order to keep silence, the ground of being, away? Aren't we seeking to forget ourselves with these forms of entertainment that occupy and cover up silence? Isn't that what we're really doing?

It's one thing to be entertained by something, and quite another to be distracted by something. It is our motivation and intent for engaging in these behaviors that determines whether these activities are healthy or not – and whether or not they're engaged in for the sake of pure enjoyment, or for the sake of running away from something we'd rather not face. Don't we already intuitively know that *we are* silence? Don't we already know that silence is an aspect or quality of who we are that never leaves us? Don't we know that it's an integral part of our experience, and that without it, we'd probably go mad? Can you even imagine a world without silence? I can't, nor do I want to.

Are you still present when thought and feeling disappear? You most certainly are. Doesn't that tell you that you can't possibly be your thoughts and feelings? Are you still present when the mind is completely still, like in meditation or deep sleep? You most certainly are. Doesn't that tell you that you can't possibly *be* the mind? Wisdom sees that when we run from the silence that we already are, silence must chase us. Wisdom sees running from what we can't ever escape only brings unnecessary pain and suffering.

It's not that silence is problematic. It's that in the silence, we are very aware of the thoughts that race around in our minds, so we go to great lengths to distract ourselves from that disturbing experience. If we'd just relax into the silence we already are, we'd see that silence is indeed golden. There is more wisdom in listening to the silence, and being receptive to silence, than there is in reading *everything* anyone has ever written or said about silence. Find this out for yourself and be free. Make friends with silence and discover that is has ALWAYS been your trusted friend all along.

Don't believe the thoughts in your head *about* silence. None of them are true. They only *feel* true, and become true for you, if you believe them. Notice all along, you've been running from the thoughts you have about things; you've been running from the thoughts you have about yourself. Stop mixing the two and wake up to what you really are. Beliefs, opinions and perceptions are all objects in your awareness. You are the subject that is aware *of* them. The Christian Trappist Monk, Thomas Merton said:

"Words stand between silence and silence: between the silence of things and the silence of our own being, between the silence of the world and silence of God. When we have really met and known the world in silence, words do not separate us from the world nor from other men, nor

*from God, nor from ourselves because we no longer trust
entirely in language to contain reality."*

Chapter 6
You Are What You Want

*"Why run around sprinkling holy water? There's an ocean inside you, and when you're ready, you'll drink." ~ **Kabir***

Imagine a world where every human woke up one day, realizing that they already were what they wanted? And that they finally saw they were living their lives like a dog chasing its tail, exhausting themselves with fruitless attempts to claim what was already theirs by birthright. As a result, there wouldn't be a whole lot of seeking going on anymore.

113

Can you imagine the implications? Wouldn't there naturally be great relief and a lightness of energy experienced? Wouldn't we have a much more joyous human race if we knew we lacked nothing at all? We would, as a whole, experience much less suffering and strife.

Since we no longer saw each other as separate anymore, we'd naturally love and accept each other. Would that be a world you'd want to live in? I sure would. In fact, there are many who've realized this, but for whatever reason, they are in the vast minority. If we desire a world where peace and love isn't just a conceptual idea – but is actually realized and expressed – then don't we have a responsibility to wake up to the reality that we already *are* what we seek? If it isn't our responsibility, whose is it? If not now, when?

Would you consider that a worthy endeavor, one that may take a bit of earnest attention to realize? What would you give for this? Would you give up all your ideas, beliefs and cherished opinions for the opportunity to realize that you are what you want? Although it may appear a scary and absurd notion, nothing less will do. Not knowing we already are what we want is the human condition. It's not accidental or haphazard that it is this way. Why? Simply because it *is* this way!

Remember, truth is simple. It's the mind's role to complicate things and turn them into complexities.

Seeking and wanting implies that we don't already possess that which we seek or want. *Just because we believe we don't possess a thing, does it actually mean we don't possess that thing?* Can we really make that assumptive leap? Just because our minds tell us we wouldn't be seeking a thing if we had it, does it make it so?

For example, do you really believe that you have a limited or finite amount of love in your heart? Do you really believe (in reality, in truth) that you don't have enough love in your heart for the entire human race - and for all the creatures, both on land and sea, and in the sky? If you don't, let me be the first to tell you: You are mistaken. I hope I didn't just offend you; that is the last thing I want to do here. But I just can't support that belief, so I must take the risk of offending you. Just because you may feel, believe or think that you don't possess enough love in your heart for all of creation doesn't make it true.

Now, I am aware that some people have had traumatic and unloving pasts, sometimes with horrific things done to them. This often leads to justifying hearts closing down, but that still doesn't equate to the truth of NOT having enough love in their hearts for all of creation, does it? Real love, true love - the kind without any condition - is present in all of us, right now. Past experience or present circumstance matters not.

The fact that many of us don't realize this doesn't alter this truth one bit. In fact, you were born with this capacity (or space in your heart) to love and embrace all of creation. Notice that I am using the words "space" and "capacity," and not using the word "potential" here. I *am* saying that this total and absolute love is already present within you right now, the kind that includes absolutely everything, without any distinction or preference. It's simply covered over by past fears, hurts, traumas and the like. Therefore, the experiences that you've accumulated over a lifetime, both good and bad, cannot harm or touch this capacity.

This unharmed, untouched "enough room in your heart already" condition is present in you, regardless of your thoughts or feelings about it. All it takes is a thought believed in to close our hearts down. Actually, hearts don't close; they are always radiating love and openness. There's no such thing as a "wounded heart". When minds are closed, hearts *feel* closed and wounded. If we close down to all, or most of the love present within us, then yes, we will feel (and even proclaim to the high heavens) that in no way do we have enough love within us for all of God's creation. Sadly, we may even conclude that if we don't have this love of self, how can we possibly have it for all of creation?

But again, does this make it true? Does this make it actually so? And how could you ever know this is true? Just because you don't feel it is so – just because you don't presently *feel* that love for all of creation? Here I am, some guy you don't personally know, saying that you already are what you want, and that you already are what you seek. Who am I to say this, you may ask? I am simply just someone who realized this many years ago desiring to spread the good news. I am simply someone who knows that, although I appear separate and distinct from you, I *am* you.

More specifically, the essence of what you are, what animates the body and mind *you* have is the very same essence animating my body and mind – and every other body and mind. Our bodies are indeed separate, distinct and different, but what animates and informs them isn't separate at all. What animated and informed Jesus, the Buddha, and Mohammed was also this one essence. We all have different intellectual capacity, different values and interests, but what animates and informs absolutely everything and everyone is the same singular essence.

Let's take less of a bite here and look at this differently, and on a smaller scale. Would you agree that in our deepest honesty, it is human nature to desire to love oneself unconditionally – and then love others in the same way? Would you also agree that, it is in fact the human condition that many of us have a real struggle with self-love, and therefore, difficulty with truly loving another? Isn't this what we most struggle with? And if this is so, don't we often go looking for love *because* we feel it's lacking within us?

Don't we have a tendency to seek out what we think we don't already have? Yes, we most certainly do. If you knew and realized that you were already the source of all that you sought, would you feel lack, limitation and angst? Would you seek these things outside of yourself? No, of course you wouldn't. Do you believe this is "pie in the sky stuff" reserved for the "lucky" few, or is there something within you right now that knows, on some level, beyond belief, that what I'm saying points to the truth ... that you already possess (in full) that which you want, that which you seek?

If you *do* think this is "pie in the sky stuff," does that make it so? It IS if you say it is. That's literally all it takes. We give untrue thoughts life all the time. It feels real in our experience, but it doesn't make it real. One unexamined thought can separate the worlds apart. And if you do think this is pie in the sky stuff, will you write it off as something unworthy of your attention? Will you continue to live your life believing what brings true fulfillment is outside of yourself, and therefore, only attained through a rigorous, looking "out there" search?

If you've noticed, there is common thread throughout these pages, and one in which can't ever be overvalued or overstated. It is a willingness to find out for yourself what is true in your own experience.

This is our aim. It is a voluntary suspension of what we *think* we know, coupled with a deep curiosity and investigation of what we hold as true. A willingness *not* to know what is true, until we *can* know, is essential. A willingness to see that not knowing is very peaceful and spacious place to be, and not something to be feared or ashamed of, is waiting to be discovered.

The other night, I was watching "Wicked Tuna" on the National Geographic channel. I had no idea these fish can weigh over 1,000lbs, grow up to twelve feet long and swim over 45 mph! Incredible. Anyway, one of the boats was fishing for tuna off the coast of Gloucester, Massachusetts. Along came a bigger, fishing vessel trolling for all types of fish, not just tuna. This vessel had a big net that was being dragged about fifty feet below the surface, ensnaring and accumulating all sorts of fish. In the process, it also snagged the anchor line of one of the tuna fishing boats, rendering it powerless and dependent for a time. I couldn't help but notice that this is the way we are as humans.

As we live our lives, we collect and assimilate all kinds of beliefs, ideas and opinions – most of which don't originate from within – and we too, become powerless and dependent for a time, sometimes for a lifetime. We take on, and scoop up, these ideas from outside sources – and act as if they are true. Somewhere along the way, we picked up the idea that not knowing means we are stupid or less than, when the opposite is actually true. All these stories are illusory and constitute our "anchor" that's snagged in the net.

Somewhere along the way, we picked up the idea that to reach out and ask for help means we're weak, when somewhere inside we know the opposite is true. It is wisdom that admits when it doesn't know, and it is wisdom that admits when it needs support. Only when it is admitted that we don't know (or that we can use a helping hand) can another possibility arise for us. We'll never live outside the confines of the box if we continue to think inside the box. This is what wisdom "demands," and this is when wisdom blooms.

Wisdom also sees that to not know is to know. We know that we don't know. That's huge, and something that's way undervalued and unappreciated in our culture! *When we know that we don't know, we are no longer deluding ourselves. When we don't delude ourselves, we allow something else to move through us. No longer are we pretending to know, because we finally have the courage to tell the truth.* With this orientation, imagine yourself standing in a room in a very dark house called, "I am what I want, I am what I seek."

The room is dark and you can't see. In order to see, you light a lantern, illuminating the room you're in. At *that* moment, just before you lit the lantern, you didn't know, you didn't see, and that was perfectly okay with you. After it was lit, you still didn't know, but you were much better equipped to see what was true or not, to see what was in the room. Because you turned on the light of awareness, you're better equipped to see how many cracks were on the walls and ceilings (labels that lie, unquestioned beliefs and assumptions) and what kind of floors were present. Your light of awareness (the lantern) instantly dispelled the darkness, and enables you to investigate each room (each aspect of yourself) in the house.

As the light is on, you notice something telling you (innate wisdom that knows) it's okay to admit to yourself you don't know, that you really *don't* see that you already are what you want – and that you're willing to keep looking to see if it is true or not. Besides, you have a sense that seeing this could be very significant. That's integrity, and that's the spirit in which all good things come. It also happens to be the orientation that eventually allows us to see what we don't presently see, allowing us to experience what we don't presently experience.

Otherwise, we're just being phony, and the phonies don't ever get to see what's really true. Phonies don't get enlightened, and phonies certainly aren't looking in the right direction. Those who engage in self-deception look for shortcuts that lead to the easier, less truthful way. The problem is, this way doesn't reveal what you really want anyway. Telling the truth isn't something to fear anymore – because like silence, truth is definitely our friend – and ultimately, what sets us free. If something *can* set us free, how can that something *not* be our friend? Why fear a real and true friend? If there is still some fear present, we don't let that stop us because we know it isn't based in what's really true anyway.

Truth isn't to be feared. It's when we believe the fears our minds fabricate (about what we have to give up or lose in order to realize that truth) that barriers arise. The mind has NO IDEA, but it thinks it does – and then we believe it! Anything we project will be seen to be true for us, because we'll imagine and create the scenario we cooked up. Then we'll conclude it was needed all along! How's that for a self-fulfilling prophecy?

In reality, it's just a random bunch of thoughts we've collected with our nets that we've come to believe and identify with. Nevertheless, just because we see them in our nets doesn't mean we're obligated to bring them on board, does it? We can let them go; we can release them back from where they came because we *see* they don't serve us. Why would we hold on to a thought that tells us we're inferior, when all it does is make us self-conscious in front of others? Instead of really questioning what specific evidence tells us this, many of us often remain stuck, acting as if it's just a "fact" of our lives.

However, if we are sincere in finding what's really so, the answer will be revealed to us. Remember, the false cannot stand up to examination! It can become a new habit – a new way of being. As long as we are open and receptive to being okay with whatever arises, it's almost always rewarding. If we truly have a desire to look at this concept that says, "You are what you want," then we must want to know the truth more than we want to feel good. If we don't, we set ourselves up for failure at the first sign of trouble.

Like the weather, feelings come and go – and therefore, are impermanent. When we place a high value and priority on that which comes and goes, we set ourselves up for disappointment and suffering, every time. When we place a high priority on that which must erode and wash away any time stormy weather appears, any time challenging situations present themselves, we set ourselves up for disillusionment and disappointment. If feeling good is our primary concern, we won't ever have the capacity or willingness to take the road less traveled, the road that ultimately leads to freedom. Seeking truth isn't always a smooth ride, and can play with our emotions.

Sometimes seeing through illusion is painful and sometimes it's a great relief. We must consciously decide that we're willing to face whatever comes our way, especially since we aren't ultimately satisfied with the status quo. If it really was that easy, so many have would have already taken that road and reported back on how easy it is! It *is* simple, but not always easy. This road does take a certain amount of courage – acting in spite of the fear, but it does lead to the Kingdom of Heaven. We must be sincere, and we must genuinely *want* to see what we don't presently see.

It is the unknown that we must enter, without any expectation or agenda. Expectations and agendas only obscure seeing what's true. Feeling good must be secondary, because we see that, like thoughts and experiences, feelings come and go – and are not to be grasped at or held onto – because they can't be grasped or held onto! Despite our past conditioning that places such importance and value on feelings being such accurate barometers for what's true and real, we see them for what they are – just energy of emotion, spontaneously arising as a result of how we're presently perceiving a person, place, thing, or situation.

When feeling good isn't our primary concern, we can defer to how the moment is actually unfolding, and not how we want it to unfold. When our focus is on feeling good, we can't help but try and manipulate our experience to suit our needs – so we feel good – and it never works in an authentic way.

It's a manufactured feeling, not an organic one. Thus, it can't last. When we're able to fully show up in this moment, it means we come naked and free, without expectation or insistence of our way being manifested.

So what do most of us really want? Whether it's realized or not, most of us seek the feeling of inner peace and self-love. We want to experience a sense of belonging and communion with others. A feeling sense of being at home wherever we are, and a feeling of being content in our own skin is what we want. Humans want physical security. In fact, it's a major driving force, and sometimes, the very thing that takes up most of our attention and concern – often to the point of obscuring the direct realization of seeing that we already are the peace and love we want. This isn't a bad thing, it just is. However, when it takes up most of our focus and attention, we have little left for seeing what's real and true.

But most of all, whether we realize it or not, we want Truth. *Essentially, every desire we have is a desire to come home, to realize and experience the wholeness and completeness that we already are.* Naturally, we seek what we don't think we possess, but at what point do we stop and say, "Hey, wait a minute, I'm not really getting anywhere; I'd better look at where I'm looking." Sadly, this recognition and stopping never happens for many of us. We go to our graves without ever really singing our song. We go to our graves never realizing who we really are.

We all want to realize the truth of who we really are, and then to live from that realization. Not conceptually, but experientially. However, when we set it up in our experience that we must have physical security in order to have inner peace, self-love and a sense of deep connection, odds are we won't ever realize we already are what we want. Truth demands all of it. If you put off feeling good as your primary concern, I can tell you this: If you look until you see, no matter what feelings arise, you'll have so many good feelings later on. They will naturally arise later, if your primary concern is discovering that you already are what you want, now.

Granted, this is easier said than done. But it doesn't take away from the fact of its simplicity. Besides, what's our alternative? If we want to see that we already are what we want – and live from that realization, that desire to see must be stronger than our need for security. I remember long ago reading Deepak Chopra saying that, security, both emotional and physical, is an illusion that can be taken away at any moment. Further, it isn't even real to begin with! I didn't believe him. Instead, I found out for myself. Deepak was right.

While it isn't always easy to see formless, intangible and invisible things like thoughts, beliefs and perceptions *as* illusory, it's not only very possible to do so, it's within our capabilities. Our direct experience, instantly, or over time, will reveal to us whether something can be relied on or not, and whether it's real or not. Our bodies will reveal to us the validity of anything in the form of flow, resonance, ease, peace, lightness, dissonance, being stuck, anxiousness, heaviness, etc. And so, when we *see* that our beliefs don't hold up through examination, or prove to have any supporting evidence, they often dissolve. What's true can't dissolve.

When we see anything as bogus, it drops away on its own. With our *seeing*, we just took the life energy away – and it dies. Have you noticed that nothing in our experience remains, and everything goes? Once this is seen, we can just control what we can control – and let the rest go. It doesn't mean that we don't plan for the future, or work towards living in comfort for our remaining days. It means that we do these things today, we plan these things today, without allowing our minds to run amok by projecting unwanted visions of an imagined future we don't want.

We pay attention to the needs of this day – and it is always *this* day. When the next day arrives, God willing, we pay attention to that day – which is *this* day. If we find this difficult, we can *return to sender* and say, "thanks for sharing, but I am staying in the endless present moment, the only reality." If we are meant to have food in our stomach, a roof over our head, and money in the bank *any* day, then it will be so. If not, we may indeed have a different experience. Either way, anticipating and fearing an imagined future (we don't want) can only intensify the possibility of it manifesting. This is critical to see.

In Matthew 6:24-34, Jesus said, *"Consider the lilies of the field, how they grow; they neither toil or spin; yet I tell you, even Solomon in all his glory was not arrayed like one of these. But if God so clothes the grass of the field, which today is alive and tomorrow is thrown into the Ocean, will he not much more clothe you, O men of little faith? And which of you by being anxious can add one cubit to his span of life?"* Listening to, and taking to heart the wisdom of Jesus when he said, "Give us this day our daily bread" ... we are grateful for our daily bread, without concern for tomorrow's bread.

What is *bread*, but the very staple of life and symbol of all that we need to live and grow? "Anxiety is neither helpful nor necessary. It robs us of faith and confidence in God's help, and it saps our energy for doing good works. Put away your petty preoccupations for material things and instead seek first the things of God – his kingdom and righteousness." As we only ever get to live one day at a time, we live for today without fearing an undesired tomorrow. Wisdom sees that tomorrow isn't even guaranteed, and that now is the only reality. If we really are what we want and seek, then why is this truth so foreign to so many of us?

The 14th Century Christian mystic, Meister Eckhart once said, *"The eye with which I see God is the same eye with which God sees me."* If this is so, why don't more of us see and enjoy the glorious implications of this beautiful truth? For starters, we were never shown this, and we are rarely among those that have realized this. Lastly, it takes an earnest desire to question everything we think we know, and everything we cherish. Not many are willing to do this! With the invention of the Internet, it's not difficult to find these people anymore. These people are out there in the world. They are mostly very ordinary, humble and unassuming people. They could very well be your next-door neighbor, the clerk at the grocery store, or your house painter.

So take heart, it isn't anyone's fault that this is the way it is. Asking "why" this is so is just an attempt by the mind to understand and control. There is no why; it just is. There's nothing wrong with seeking out these people, whether it's on the Internet, your local bookstore or in your local community, *as you look within to confirm this truth in your being.* In fact, I suggest it. Remember, wisdom sees the good sense of using crutches for a time, until one can walk on their own. As the Zen saying proclaims, *"If the truth isn't right where you are, where else do you expect to find it?"* Truth, being present all the time, doesn't come and go.

Find out what you are, find out what doesn't come and go, and enjoy your life. Feelings, thoughts and perceptions are all objects in your awareness that come and go, so they can't be what you are. The activity of thinking, an object in your awareness, comes and goes. That can't be what you are, either. What you ARE is eternally present, and prior to all that comes and goes – and is the ground of being. Find out what remains, when all else doesn't, and the ballgame is over. The great Indian Sage, Ramana Maharshi once said, *"Let what comes come and let what goes go. Find out what remains."*

There is something so elusively obvious that I must mention it here. We've all had the experience of looking for something that we've misplaced. Perhaps it's our car keys we thought we placed on the table, or the pickle jar that we could have sworn we still had in the fridge. We search and search, but can't seem to find them. Eventually we give up and sit down, dumbfounded that they're nowhere in sight. All of sudden, they appear out of nowhere, sitting right there on the edge of the coffee table, or staring right at us from the top shelf of the fridge, where we suspected it was all along. They were never truly lost; they just appeared to be lost. We just didn't see them.

Similarly, when we assume or believe that we aren't already the truth, love or peace that we want, we are missing something so obvious that it *seems* elusive. Therefore, we conclude it isn't already present! Asking the right questions is critical if we are to discover what's true. Asking the right questions orients us to look in the direction where truth reveals itself.

When we assume we aren't what we seek, we fail to ask ourselves a few pertinent and revealing questions: Is the love that I want and that I seek, not already present in my experience, right now? Is the inner peace that I want and seek, not already present in my experience, right now? Now, you may not feel or sense the love and peace directly (and immediately) when you ask these questions, but don't allow that temporary experience make you draw the lasting conclusion that you aren't already what you seek!

I can assure you this: If you were to get quiet and sit in silence for a few minutes, days, months (or for however long it takes YOU) then that which you want will reveal itself as that which was never absent. If you're earnest, and you want it more than you want to feel good, it will reveal itself beyond the chatter of the mind, without any doubt or confusion. If at first you don't succeed, try again. If at first it doesn't reveal itself within your preferred timetable, keep looking. The fact is, it could care less about your timetable. It only cares about your sincere looking above all else. Your fears and apprehension don't matter. Bring them with, as you look. Don't wait for them to disappear, or you may wait forever.

Resist the temptation of believing you must take a journey to see this, and that it must take *time* to see this. It can literally happen for you in an instant, even right now. Drop all agendas and preferences and allow for anything to happen; allow for all of it to happen, in *its* way, not *your* way. Your agenda is totally irrelevant. If you make this finding your number one priority, above all else, you won't be a seeker forever. And when you do find, you won't regret any of the experiences you've ever had, nor will you be anxious of any future happening to come. Both will drop away. You'll finally know what Jesus really meant when he talked about being one with the Father, and what he really meant when he referenced the Kingdom of Heaven.

When you turn up the light up conscious awareness, go within, and finally meet yourself, you'll recognize that the love you've been seeking was (all along) right where you are – IS what you are. You'll recognize you never had to go out in search of it. Always start where you are. This fire has been lit all along and has been burning brightly. It's never been extinguished, even for a moment. Once you see this, you can then be a light unto others. As the Buddha once said, *"First be a light unto yourself."* Stop looking for blessings and be the blessing you already are.

There is a wonderful story that illustrates this point. You may have heard of it because it is a timeless classic called, "Acres of Diamonds," about a farmer who lived in Africa and through a visitor, became tremendously excited about looking for diamonds. Diamonds were already discovered in great abundance on the African continent and this farmer became so enthralled with the idea of acquiring millions of dollars worth of diamonds that he sold his farm to go out in search of these diamonds. He searched and searched the continent over and as the years slipped by, his exhaustive search turned up empty. Eventually he went completely broke, and in despair, threw himself into a river and drowned.

Meanwhile, the new owner of his farm came across an unusual looking rock about the size of an egg and placed it on his mantle as a decorative piece. A visitor dropped by one day and upon seeing the rock, became so excited he started jumping up and down. He told the new owner of the farm that the rock on his mantle was perhaps the largest diamond that had ever been found.

The new owner of the farm said, "Well, the whole farm is covered with them" – and sure enough it was. The farm turned out to be the Kimberly Diamond Mine, the richest the world has ever known. The original farmer was literally sitting on "acres of diamonds" until he sold his farm. Each of us is right smack in the middle of our own "acres of diamonds", if only we would realize it and develop the ground we are standing on before charging off in search of greener pastures. Is the love that I seek not already present right here, right now? Is the inner peace that I seek not already present right here, right now – before I go in search of it? Is Truth not already present before I go out in search of it?

Osho said, *"Drop the idea of becoming someone, because you are already a masterpiece. You cannot be improved. You have only to come to it, to know it, to realize it."*

Chapter 7
The Greatest Gift You Can Give

"What is true is already so. Owning up to it doesn't make it worse. Not being open about it doesn't make it go away. And because it's true, it is what is there to be interacted with. Anything untrue isn't there to be lived. People can stand what is true, for they are already enduring it."

~ Eugene Gendlin

There is a peculiar and consistent phenomenon that human consciousness reveals. And it is this: Consciousness has a real tendency to forget that to be human is to be possessed with both strengths *and* weaknesses. We forget that human nature is, by nature, bound by time and limited by sensory perception. To deny these facts is to deny our very humanity. Failing to see that, by design, we are created with both a limited and unlimited nature, we often judge and condemn. In so doing, we cement the notion that perfection is a human potential, when in truth, it's merely an idea we've been taught to chase after, an idea that if attained would make us happier.

The fortunate few recognize that, in that chasing, "perfection" is always a moving target – and one that can never be attained. Throughout the ages, saints, sages and the mystics alike have expressed this experience of "not rightness" as a sense of being off kilter, off balance, fractured, broken or divided. The Buddha proclaimed in the first of his Four Noble Truths that "Life is suffering" – and to be mindful that suffering arises when we fail to include absolutely everything in our experience, not just what we *want* in our experience.

In my book, *"The Dance of Imperfection – Living in Perfect Harmony with Life,"* we re-examine our interpretations of what it means to be imperfect – and how those interpretations impact our experience.

Ralph Waldo Emerson said, *"There is a crack in everything God has made."* It is in this crack (what I refer to as "perceived imperfection" or simply, "weakness") – and it is through the absolute and complete acceptance of *this* crack – that wholeness reveals itself AS our true nature. Therefore, it is *in and through* that crack of imperfection where our opportunity resides, if we would just see it. It is in and through that crack of "imperfection" where our transcendence takes place.

It is only a thought believed in that tells us otherwise; it is only a thought believed in that separates the sun, the moon, the sky and the oceans. Until then, this crack of "imperfection" will continue to torture and divide, until we see the profound opportunity in each moment of our existence. When we accept ourselves with all of our strengths and weaknesses, we give ourselves the opportunity to truly show up and be supportive for another in a way that is authentic and potentially transforming.

When we realize the truth of our dual nature, we're able to embrace and include all of ourselves, not just the desired half. When we see that the inherent nature of our own limitations can't be any other way than it is – we render ourselves truly humble. It is in this recognition where we understand the nature of our situation. It is in this humility and understanding where we're able to be of real service to those in need. When we no longer *unconsciously (and ignorantly) point out in others that which we don't love and accept about ourselves,* we're then in a position to truly be a catalyst for a new potential.

Then and only then, are we really able to be a neutral sounding board for another who seeks a way out of their present situation. Then and only then, are we really able to truly be an agent for change – if change is desired. Wisdom sees human beings connect with each other in a meaningful way in the reality of their shared weaknesses, and not so much on the basis of common strengths. It is in this vulnerability and acknowledgement of our shared weakness that makes us alike; it is in our strengths where we're different.

Where we most connect and heal is in a space of mutual recognition and shared acceptance of our accepted limitations. We all struggle with varying demons, fears and personal grief, while doing the best we can with what we have. We are all "imperfectly perfect," or "perfectly imperfect" just the way we are. It is this unabashed acknowledgement of our dual nature that gives us the wherewithal to live our lives with self-honesty and dignity. Pretenders won't see this. Those unwilling to face themselves as they are won't see this. It is this self-honesty and willingness to face ourselves as we are right now, that creates a rooted connectedness with others that bind; these are the "ties that bind."

Like each wave in the ocean appears separate from other waves – but remains the same ocean, we are one and the same, despite appearing to be different and separate. Expressing our unique strengths and abilities, we naturally grow in different ways and directions, while maintaining the exact same source and substance of who we really are. We remain rooted in the same soil of our own down to earth and humble imperfection. And it is in *this* fertile soil that wisdom blooms. It is in *this* fertile soil where we live more from what we "know" is true, and less from what we "believe" is true.

The willingness not to know what's actual can never be overvalued. In fact, wisdom sees that not knowing is often the only appropriate response to a situation. When it comes to another's struggle, we are aware that to offer unsolicited advice may be equal to robbing them of what they need to experience for themselves. Regardless of the urge we may feel to give advice, no matter how helpful we think it may be, we just can't know what is the highest good for another. How can we know, unless we listen to our mind that might tell us what's best for another? Recognizing this, I won't try to impose my will on you, or anyone else.

Instead, I want to welcome you, just as you are. That's real love. Real love that comes from wholeness provides and engenders the space for something quite different to start informing our activities. Unless we're asked, real love lets you find your own way, in your time, because it's about you, not me. With our shared weaknesses as the common thread in the human experience, we can appreciate (and even be grateful for) another's strengths *and* weaknesses, rather than be intimidated by them. Sometimes the best and most appreciated thing we could ever say to another struggling is nothing at all. Just our nonjudgmental and compassionate presence conveys so much more than any words we can ever say.

This brings up a metaphor for me. Most men don't want to admit when they're lost, especially when they have a woman in the car with them. And if it's a new woman in their lives they want to impress, forget about it. No way, no how, are they stopping at a gas station to get directions! They will drive around, even in circles, attempting to give the impression that they KNOW where they're going. They'll attempt to convey that they're just "temporarily turned around" and not to worry because everything is still under control.

In fact, for as long as they can pull it off, most men will go to great lengths to continue the facade that they know where they're headed. They'd rather drive around for hours, lost, rather than swallow their pride and ask for directions. Arriving on time takes a backseat to the show they must put on. And the funny thing is, the woman almost always knows he's lost, but the man's need for keeping up the charade has a tendency to delude him into thinking he's successfully hiding the fact he's lost. Personally, I can't relate to this, as I've never done this. Yeah right – and I have some swampland in Florida for sale that you'll love; no alligators or crocodiles included, either!

My Mom loves to tell the story of how I got lost once (13 years ago, mind you) probably because she is well aware of the male ego's need to always know where he's headed! Anyway, with my destination ten hours due West, I somehow found myself traveling North for two hours before I realized I was heading in the wrong direction! Thirteen years later, there's still a response that says, "Hey, what are you talking about – I've got a great sense of direction" when she insists on telling the story! Today, it's much easier for me to pull over and ask for directions when I need to – but Mom, I still have a pretty good sense of direction!

Invariably, if you ask a man for directions when *you're* lost, he's usually happy to tell *you* how to get there. If he has a woman in the car with him, he's even more eager to assist. Aren't we naturally happy to give directions to a complete stranger who's lost? I mean, how many of us think, "Oh crap, what a pain this nimrod is; I've got better things to do right now than give this guy or gal directions." Not many of us. It makes us feel good to point the way to others who are lost.

It makes us feel good to give directions to those who have lost their way. It may even be a subtle ego boost for us, giving us the opportunity to take credit for being able to assist someone in need. After all, we "know" the way and they don't. There's just something about giving guidance to another human being that feels satisfying. Women aren't immune to this by any means. In many ways, women are more willing to be helpful, and their motives may be a bit less ego-driven than men. It may seem that I'm making hasty generalizations here – and perhaps I am, but I'm simply trying to illustrate a point.

While it is very easy and natural for all of us to *give* directions, we often find it very difficult and unnatural to *ask for and receive* directions. All those years I was reading books and listening to tapes about spirituality, for some reason I just wouldn't look long enough in the directions I was being pointed. I may have glanced, but I certainly never looked until I saw. Consequently, I remained stuck in most of the same challenges I was facing.

We can conveniently chalk it up to the male ego as being the primary reason men generally have a more difficult time asking for direction – or looking in the direction suggested – but let's delve deeper and see if there might be more to it than that. There's something peculiarly consistent and predictable about human consciousness – male or female – when it comes to receiving direction from another. We generally don't want it because we think we know what's best for us. In our lack of humility, we don't want guidance because we conclude if we need outside help, it must mean we're weak. Coming from ego, how else *can* we feel?

This conclusion goes unquestioned, like so many other beliefs and assumptions we have. Our world can be falling apart all around us, yet we rarely consider examining the beliefs and assumptions we operate from. The truth is, wisdom knows that to admit we don't know is anything *but* weak. If we truly desire to be free, we must see that it's ALL an inside game – and that nothing outside of us can ever harm us without our consent.

Therefore, never are we a victim, unless we *play* the victim. Seeing that we are the final authority in our own experience (and that nobody can define who we are) is essential if we are to experience the "peace that surpasses all understanding" – the peace that never goes away, regardless of circumstance. Belief won't do this, only realization will.

Even though we are the final authority, wisdom sees the benefit of looking where another points, especially if that other has realized what we are looking for. Nevertheless, we are the only one who can confirm for ourselves what's actual in our experience. Second-hand knowledge or opinion is fruitless. Generally speaking, unless we specifically ask for advice and direction, we don't really want it.

Isn't this true in *your* experience, especially if it's unsolicited? How many of us actually welcome unsolicited advice from others, the kind that implies "you should be different than you are?"

Don't we almost always feel a cringing contraction upon hearing advice? We sure do – and the primary reason is this: the message being sent to us is we need to be fixed; we need to change because the way we are right now just isn't "right." In short, we should be different than we are – and thus, we can't be appreciated for the *way* we are. For example, I remember being told by a college friend many years ago that I said, "Who cares" a lot – and it bothered him quite a bit, and I knew it.

His assertion initially stung me, but later on I realized why. I saw that when it came to my relationship with him, it was true. I did say, "Who cares" quite a bit. There was a part of me that didn't like my attitude, especially since I saw myself as a caring person. My motive was to annoy him because I *knew* it bothered him. However, on closer examination, I noticed that the driving force wasn't that I simply wanted to annoy him, but rather, that I didn't appreciate him calling me out on a number of other things *he* deemed unacceptable and annoying in *me*.

Consequently, I wanted him to know that I wasn't hearing or acknowledging his judgments of me by saying, "who cares?" I didn't appreciate his condemnation and judgment. Today I'm sure I'd handle it differently, but it's where I was at the time. Thinking we need to point out to others what's "not right" about them, and suggesting ways in which they can improve themselves or their situation only alienates us from each other. Even worse, thinking it's *our* responsibility to point out how others can change only divides, and never unites. We fail to consider walking in another's shoes before we go doling out advice.

There's no real wisdom in division, only in unity. In certain circumstances we could certainly debate this. However, when it comes to connection with another, and being supportive of another, wisdom always resides in inclusion, not division. Even if our intentions are "good," taking the liberty to point out to another how they can improve rarely ends up being received in a way that's welcomed, or in a way that actually transforms and enlightens. Identified with ego, it's natural to be attached to conveying our "great wisdom." But who wants to feel like they need to be rescued or fixed? Who wants to feel as if they're being perceived as an incompetent fool - a project that needs desperate repair?

Only when a person is open and willing to hear an outside perspective, can a positive and lasting impact be made. Only when someone is openly receptive to feedback - or has *asked for* that feedback -

are they ready to *hear* and benefit from that feedback – because they've put themselves in a space where change can occur. Only when a person is ready and willing to see what's really so, and move beyond where they are – and not rely on belief – will they have the courage to look where they're being pointed.

Any time we condemn or judge another, we send the message (and restricting energy) they need to change or be fixed. We impregnate them with ignorance. Thus, we resist reality. It's a lose-lose situation – for both of us.

So what does all this have to do with wisdom blooming and awakening the sage within, you might be thinking? Well, everything actually. Any time we're acting out of ignorance, we're naturally suppressing wisdom. Any time we're acting from wisdom, we're naturally suppressing ignorance. Any time we remain in the grips of fear, and aren't willing to look in the direction of truth, we're suppressing our natural wisdom. If what we do to others, we also do to ourselves, it follows that we can never escape the energetic shaping component of how we perceive others, the words we speak to others, and the approach we take with others. This energetic component ultimately either enslaves or liberates.

In other words, if we convey to others that they need to change, be fixed or saved, we confirm within ourselves that at some point we needed to change, be fixed or saved, too. On closer examination, we notice that ignorance sees that repair is necessary, while wisdom sees that everything is absolutely okay as it is. Wisdom knows that whenever we hold back another, we hold ourselves back. Wisdom won't bloom because the energetic soil isn't properly prepared. Judgment, criticism and condemnation, all ignorant energies, carry a constricting energy. These energies naturally "dry up" the soil, and remove all the necessary nutrients and minerals for wisdom to bloom.

Allow me to repeat this very essential point: Don't believe a word you read here. Everything you read here – or anywhere else – is merely conceptual and only points to something else, but can be confirmed and validated in your own direct experience. The word is never the thing.

Does your intuition tell you that there is such a thing as *"the way things shouldn't be?"* I invite you to simply stop, and just be with this notion for a whole thirty seconds before reading on. (Right now, the "Jeopardy" song is playing while you do this.) Okay, what came up for you? Does it make any sense to you that there is such a thing as the way things shouldn't be? Have you ever really examined this widely held viewpoint that informs the majority of our moment-to-moment experience? What does it really mean when we tell ourselves that things or people shouldn't be the way they are? Have we ever really contemplated how this viewpoint shapes our experience?

What are we essentially telling ourselves when we decide things like, "It shouldn't be this way," "This person shouldn't be this way" or "These circumstances shouldn't be this way?" Are *any* of these instances ever true? Can they EVER be true? In our insistence that a particular person, thing or circumstance shouldn't be the way they are – or the way it is, aren't we basically saying that WE are the final judge, jury *and* executioner of the universe – and that nature, the universe (or God) has it all wrong? Isn't this perspective full of self-righteousness and arrogance?

Wouldn't the main culprit then, be ignorance – the direct opposite of wisdom – that compels us to *be* arrogant and self-righteous? And yet, we do this all the time, don't we? We don't wake up each morning and decide to be this way; it just happens this way for most of us. Why? Simply because we're not aware – we're not conscious of what's going on. This is an observation and NOT a judgment, by the way. It makes sense that if we knew better we'd do better. Put another way, things can only be the way they are because whatever is can only come from the consciousness (or level of awareness) that manifested it.

Naturally, if we were more conscious, we'd live more in harmony with the flow of life. Life isn't insane, we are. Reality doesn't resist what is; we do. As I like to remind, "In order to understand, we must

148

first be aware." We can't ever understand what we're not first aware of. Therefore, it follows that when we come from ignorance – the opposite of wisdom, we'll maintain and believe in the "this shouldn't be" perspective. And we live in a dream.

If reality is "what is," then how can the "it shouldn't be this way" notion ever truly exist? It can't. The only thing that gives this perspective life is the mind that believes it. If it only exists in the mind – and nowhere else, it isn't real. Ultimately, what it comes down to is simply an argument with reality. And *any* time we argue with reality (what is), we suffer. Any time we oppose life and insist on "what shouldn't be," we lose. What a wonderful and reliable consistency to count on and rest in! If we're looking for ANY security at all, this is it. We can rest assured knowing that whatever presently happens (it's always the present) is meant to happen, and can't happen any other way.

Why would we ever resist reality if we want to be happy and at peace? Isn't that insane? Why would we ever CHOOSE to make ourselves unhappy? We don't choose – but we can see that this "choosing" goes on by itself. When we become conscious and see what's really happening, we "choose" different by looking in the direction that doesn't hurt and divide.

Imagine for a moment that you're taking a leisurely stroll with your lover through a wooded trail paved with beautiful stone. You come upon a rather large tree root sticking out of the ground, right up through the stone path. At the time you notice this root sticking up out of the ground, your mind decides, "This root shouldn't be here; I was peacefully enjoying a stroll with my lover along this beautiful stone path – and all of a sudden, this root is sticking out of the ground, right smack in the middle of the path." You argue with reality – the root is there – right in the middle of the path, and you don't want it there. The reality is, it's just a root.

The root has no notion of whether it *should* or *shouldn't be* there. None of this makes sense to the root. Nature has no concept of what should or "shouldn't be" – and as a result, it never suffers. Our mind decides it shouldn't be there. Since we believe it, we feel justified in our thinking and justified in our annoyance – and there goes our peace and enjoyment. No more leisurely stroll! It's a convincing closed loop that has us believing in it, for a lifetime in many cases.

In doing so, we separate ourselves from the flow of reality (the root is there) with our *thought* that it shouldn't be there. That's all it takes. And you believed thoughts weren't that powerful? Think again. Thoughts aren't really the problem. Believing in them is the problem! On the face of things, this may appear to be a silly example, but this is exactly what we do with our circumstances and experiences and with others. There's a consistent outcome when we do this: we always lose – and reality *always* wins.

Wisdom sees the ground must be fertile and ready – and the conditions properly prepared, in order for sprouting to occur.

Wisdom sees that one of the greatest gifts we can give another is to accept them for who they are, holding them in a space of absolute non-judgment and infinite potential. This is the soil that engenders real growth. Wisdom sees that there's no such thing as "this person shouldn't be this way" … and that in fact, this person can only BE the way they presently are – and *can't possibly* be any other way then they presently are. This is so simple the mind overlooks this revolutionary truth. Truth is simple. It always is. If this is true for another, it must be true for you.

Wisdom knows that since everything is vibrating energy, including thoughts, beliefs, judgments and perceptions, negation and denial can only continue to strengthen and enslave rather than dissolve and liberate. Compassion knows a message that ultimately says, "You are broken and need fixing," is both counterintuitive and counterproductive.

Conversely, the energy that releases and frees is of a total and absolute deep okay-ness with what is, as it is. Since everything is intimately connected and inseparable, this must include the way we view another's situation. Thinking or believing that we're immune from HOW we approach and view others is a great formula for continued discord for us.

When Wisdom Blooms

The wisdom of no escape mandates that if we want the best for ourselves, we must also want the best for others. If I don't come from the energetic vibrations that frees and releases, then I'm further enslaving the both of us. If I don't come *from* wisdom, I can only teach ignorance. Consequently, instead of wisdom blooming, ignorance blooms. If I don't come from wisdom, I only keep you confined, unless YOU know full well that *acceptance of your entire present lot transcends all.* Wisdom sees that we can never fool God, the universe, nature, life or whatever you prefer to call it. Only the authentic get to pass go and collect $200.

When we allow another to just be as they are, without any need to change or fix them, something lets go. Not only do we free them, we free ourselves in the process.

What's good for the goose is good for the gander. Since there's no separation, there can't be any escape, either. When we truly see this, we can stop running! Why would you EVER run from that which can only chase you? When we give another the freedom to be exactly as they are, in that giving, we give ourselves a most precious gift as well, the freedom to be who we are, exactly as we are. *Because* we held them in a space of love and acceptance (and not judgment or denial) another possibility can be stimulated and lived from.

The fundamental truth of mutuality (that pervades all realms of spirituality) holds up. While it's true that in the giving we receive, we're only able to *receive* when we are truly willing to give. We can only experience release when we have released, when *we've* let go. In so doing, we pass on this gift of release, through our energy that frees. It is a palpable and spacious feeling felt in the body and mind. Naturally, you want more of it, but wisdom sees that wanting it keeps it away. In the gap right before you seek it, you realize you are it, already. No becoming needed. In that seeing, wanting dropped away – and therefore, so did seeking.

In that seeing, the energy that's created no longer confines, but releases. Wisdom sees that when no opposition to life occurs, new possibilities can arise. When you know you already ARE what you seek, that recognition brings forth an organic experience in the body – an aliveness that doesn't come and go – confirming what you've known all along. To seek is to deny its full presence already.

What we deny in us will never blossom in us. What we face and embrace must dissolve *in* and *by* our loving gaze – and bloom eternally. When we give the gift of freedom to another, we can't help but simultaneously give ourselves the same, wonderful gift. It is in the true giving that we receive, and it is in the true receiving that we give.

We discover that the statement, "All is One" isn't just a conceptual statement to believe in, or a comforting statement to accept on faith. Instead, Oneness is something to be validated experientially. The good news is it's something we *can* validate in our experience, and is more authentic validation that all IS one – but only if we dispel ignorance with the light of awareness, and let wisdom inform us.

Absolutely everything in the manifest and un-manifested world is made of energy. Thoughts, feelings, interpretations, beliefs, trees, grass, cars, oceans, mountains, dogs, cats, food, houses and people all come from the same source. Despite it all appearing solid, nothing is solid. Absolutely everything in the manifest world flashes in and out of existence (each nanosecond, each instant) at such a high rate of speed that our senses literally cannot perceive it.

Truth is always beyond the appearance of things, and is literally never what we "think" or believe it is. What we think is, is always illusory. Quantum physics has finally caught up with what the enlightened have been conveying for centuries, and has proven that all energy is manipulated by our perception of it – how we observe it.

In other words, the observer and the observed are one. No separation. Just more validation that there is no separation, that you *are* the universe, that there is *no* escape, and that indeed, all *is* one. Wisdom blooms in this recognition - and when we live in harmony with this truth, and not just talk about it conceptually. Wisdom won't bloom when we pretend to know when we really don't. Wisdom blooms only when we go beyond the limits of conceptual understanding to the essence beneath and behind the appearance of things.

Without any judgment, denial or wishing anything was any different than it presently is, wisdom blooms because we tell the truth of our situation. No longer do we run from our experience. We face what is, as is. No sugarcoating, no hiding from, no compensating for and no rejecting. This is the spirit that transcends, the spirit that is the ground of all being, that which includes without preference or partiality. It's the ground of being that sees absolutely everything is appropriate and perfect, just the way it is. Whenever we find ourselves condemning another, we are directly faced with our own ignorance staring right back at us.

Ignorance isn't something to be avoided or ashamed of, but to be appreciated for what it is: a simple reminder that we aren't in tune with reality or truth - that our thoughts and judgments about another never define another. Instead, they are just that, thoughts and judgments about another, thoughts that define *us* as a person needing to judge. Ignorance expressed is a reminder that wisdom must arise with it, for they are two sides of the same coin.

When we resist or condemn our ignorance, we suppress our natural state of wisdom. When we embrace our ignorance, our innate wisdom blossoms. Our innate wisdom blooms when it sees that, without our ignorance, wisdom wouldn't or couldn't bloom in our experience.

Anyone who has been fortunate enough to experience a very deep, unconditional love knows that real love transcends all circumstance and experience. With this love, you can feel the walls of separation and opposition come down in the acknowledgment of a deep connection rooted in this love. When we have awakened to the kind of love that transcends all experience, good and bad, a dramatic shift occurs in our relationship with life itself. No longer are we subject to what our culture or conditioning tells us *about* love; we go beyond and experience it for ourselves.

We know that no matter how respected the authority is, we can't ever rely on what others tell us. This is the love that has no opposite, but is present through absolutely everything all the time. Jesus knew this kind of love didn't discriminate or make distinctions. Both the prostitute and the King were equally worthy of this love. This truth is timeless, and being outside the stream of time, is just as relevant today. Wisdom blooms when we allow this truth to inform the words we speak and the actions we take. The greatest gift we can give another, then, is becoming more conscious ourselves.

More specifically, the greatest gift we can give another is to become conscious of what's really true – and not just what appears to be true. Our higher consciousness impacts the entirety of consciousness, if only a little bit. If in our ignorance we can only keep down and confine, it follows that in our real wisdom that sees, we lift up and liberate. Understanding that another can never be different than they are – and the notion they "should be different than they are" is literally insane thinking. When we rightly see another, we hold both them and us in a space where something very different can begin to inform our perceptions and activities.

Something of a higher order can move in and replace what was once of a lower order – but only if the ground is fertile with the realization that what already arises can't be any different, no matter what the mind decides or perceives. Truth is always independent of, and never depends on, thinking or perceiving. Like wisdom, truth stands alone and needs no defense. Wisdom sees that things are often very different than they were, even different than they will be, but they are never different than they *are*. Wisdom blooms in the full embrace of this simple, un-deluded recognition of this reality.

Stop dreaming. Wake up from the mis-identification with the mind. Wake up from the concept of time, and be what you already are. And let wisdom bloom.

No belief necessary.

www.ingramcontent.com/pod-product-compliance
Lightning Source LLC
Chambersburg PA
CBHW070205060426
42445CB00033B/1547